Broken Memories

Remains from the Jewish cemetery in Kutno

Kutno, Poland

JewishGen

מרכז עולמי לגנאלוגיה יהודית

The Global Home for Jewish Genealogy

A Publication of JewishGen, INC
Edmond J. Safra Plaza, 36 Battery Place, New York, NY 10280
646.494.5972 | info@JewishGen.org | www.jewishgen.org

An affiliate of New York's Museum of Jewish Heritage – A Living Memorial to the Holocaust

MUSEUM OF
JEWISH HERITAGE
A LIVING MEMORIAL
TO THE HOLOCAUST

Broken Memories

Remains from the Jewish cemetery in Kutno

Kutno, Poland

Copyright © 2022 by Regional Museum of Kutno; All rights reserved
Published by JewishGen, INC.
First Printing: June 2022, Sivan 5782

Project Coordinator: Yosef Kutner
Cover Design: Rachel Kolokoff Hopper

Book content in English and Hebrew

Printed in the United States of America by Lightning Source, Inc.

Library of Congress Control Number (LCCN): 2022934814

ISBN: 978-1-954176-46-1 (hard cover: 180 pages, alk. paper)

About JewishGen.org

JewishGen, an affiliate of the Museum of Jewish Heritage - A Living Memorial to the Holocaust, serves as the global home for Jewish genealogy.

Featuring unparalleled access to 30+ million records, it offers unique search tools, along with opportunities for researchers to connect with others who share similar interests. Award winning resources such as the Family Finder, Discussion Groups, and ViewMate, are relied upon by thousands each day.

In addition, JewishGen's extensive informational, educational and historical offerings, such as the Jewish Communities Database, Yizkor Book translations, InfoFiles, Family Tree of the Jewish People, and KehilaLinks, provide critical insights, first-hand accounts, and context about Jewish communal and familial life throughout the world.

Offered as a free resource, JewishGen.org has facilitated thousands of family connections and success stories, and is currently engaged in an intensive expansion effort that will bring many more records, tools, and resources to its collections.

Please visit https://www.jewishgen.org/ to learn more.

Executive Director: Avraham Groll

About the JewishGen Press

JewishGen Press (formerly the Yizkor Books-in-Print Project) is the publishing division of JewishGen.org, and provides a venue for the publication of non-fiction books pertaining to Jewish genealogy, history, culture, and heritage.

In addition to the Yizkor Book category, publications in the Other Non-Fiction category include Shoah memoirs and research, genealogical research, collections of genealogical and historical materials, biographies, diaries and letters, studies of Jewish experience and cultural life in the past, academic theses, and other books of interest to the Jewish community.

Please visit https://www.jewishgen.org/press/ to learn more.

Director of JewishGen Press: Joel Alpert
Managing Editor - Jessica Feinstein
Publications Manager - Susan Rosin

BALTIC SEA

LITHUANIA

RUSSIA

Vilnius ●

GERMANY

POLAND

BELARUS

Kutno
●
Poznan ●

Berlin ●

Warsaw ●

Brest
●

Lodz ●

Lublin
●

● Wroclaw

● Prague

UKRAINE

● Kraków

CZECH REPUBLIC

SLOVAKIA

AUSTRIA

250 miles

250 Km   500 Km

POLAND – CURRENT BORDERS

Map of Poland with **Kuntno** indicated

BROKEN MEMORIES

Remains from the Jewish cemetery in Kutno

Hebrew – English

FOREWORD AND THANKS

The pictures of gravestones in this book have been put together from pictures of the fragments, recovered since the 1980s by the municipality of Kutno, and specifically the former directors of the Regional Museum of Kutno, the late Mr. Andrzej Urbaniak and Mr. Paweł Szymczak. Seven hundred fragments were recovered in the surroundings walls and pavement, during years of tireless work. The fragments have been cleaned, numbered, photographed and stored in a storage room in Kutno, awaiting a proper moment.

That moment came, in mid-2008, when a new group of descendants of Jews from Kutno was formed. Using computer-scanned pictures of the fragments, it was possible to put together nearly half of them into 159 more or less complete gravestones (*matzevot*). Among these, only a small part displayed a family name, as was usual on *matzevot* of that time (family names were enforced on Polish Jews at the beginning of the 19th century). For the most part, they displayed only the name of the deceased, that of his or her father, and the date of death. Comparing the *matzeva* data with that of our genealogical database, it was possible to recover some of the missing information and especially the family names. This data was added in this book.

The 'new' cemetery in Kutno was created in 1793. It existed for 150 years before it was totally destroyed, during World War II. The Nazis sought to eradicate all signs of Jewish existence in Poland – 1000 years of History and culture – and so, every piece recovered makes their defeat even more bitter. While the names of the smaller Nazi criminals have been forgotten a few years after their death, the names of our ancestors remain, thanks to the work of some enlightened people in Poland and to the vitality of Jewish passion for genealogy.

The result is this book, and an ambitious project to restore the cemetery and return the *matzevot* within its walls. This restoration will hopefully happen in the next years, with a lot of goodwill and generosity.

This book was made possible thanks to the work of Mrs Thia Persoff, who strained her eyes for weeks on barely readable *matzevot* and translated the Hebrew text into English, and to that of Mrs. Elynn Cohen who created the logo of our group – inspired from a 200-year-old stamp of the Jewish community in Kutno – and the cover illustration.

Deep thanks are also owed to Mr. Zbigniew Wdowiak, vice-president of the municipality of Kutno, and to Mrs. Katarzyna Erwińska of the Regional Museum, for their support and their dedication to the revival of Jewish culture in Poland as well as the authorization to use the pictures of the pieces of *matzevot* used in this book.

Netanya, Israel, March 2022.

Yosef Kutner

Jewish Kutno Group

LIST OF GRAVESTONES

1 – Miryam Ryvka, daughter of Chaim Yehuda, 23 January 1909
2 – Ester (ZAURBACH?), daughter of Yeshayahu (GUTMAN?)
3 – Sara, daughter of Moshe HaKohen, 3 March 1887
4 – Chaim Yosef MARKUS, son of Moshe, 10 November 1917
5 – Priwe TRUNK, daughter of Chaim NAUMBURG, wife of Gaon Israel Yehoshua, 23 October 1899
6 – Yaakov MOSZKOWICZ, son of Mordechai HaLevi
7 – Baruch Shlomo BOK, son of Abraham Yitzhak, 29 December 1915
8 – Mrs HERSZKOWICZ
9 – Ester OSOSKA, 20 October 1904
10 – Pinchas Baruch WORCEL, son of Ben Zion, 30 July 1909
11 – Moshe, son of Eliezer, 1905-1906
12 – Sheina, daughter of Shraga, 6 June 1907
13 – Shmuel Shlomo, son of Moshe (HaLevi)
14 – Moshe Aharon, son of Yitzhak, 29 April 1903
15 – Chaya Dvora, daughter of Pinchas Zelig, 18 May 1901
16 – Mordechai, son of Moshe Aharon, 29 May 1901
17 – Eliezer MANES, son of Menachem, 14 May 1885
18 – Sheindel
19 – Gitel ARONOWICZ, daughter of Israel, 17 November 1913
20 – Aharon, son of Yosef, 12 April 1899
21 – Ahuva (Liba?) FRENKIEL?, daughter of Matityahu GOLDMAN, spouse of Matys Hersh, 8 August 1909
22 – Pinchas Ze'ev Kibel?, son of Yehuda, 15 September 1894
23 – Bracha, daughter of Yehoshua Ayzik, 27 May 1870
24 – Menachem Yehuda FALC, son of Naftali Zvi, 8 April 1916
25 – ?, son of Jakob HaLevi, 12/1917 or 01/1918
26 – Sara, daughter of Moshe Dov HaKohen, 30 June 1904
27 – Eliezer KLINGBEIL, son of Chaim, 14 May 1892
28 – Anshel BIBERGAL, son of Zvi Leib, 5 July 1916
29 – Israel, son of Eli HaKohen, 18 March 1896
30 – Chana KRENIK, daughter of Akiva
31 – Israel Meir, son of Abraham, 14 March 1890
32 – Yehuda, son of Moshe, 18 November 1912
33 – (no name, man)
34 – Baruch Yitzhak ROZENCWEIG, son of Efraim, 19 November 1887
35 – Gershon, son of Yaakov, 5 September 1896
36 – Sara, daughter of Abraham, 25 January 1912
37 – Nesha, daughter of Shimon
38 – Yehuda, son of Yaakov, 26 December 1910
39 – Tauba Keila (BROD?), daughter of Moshe (MAUER?), 28 January 1871
40 – Beila, daughter of Moshe, 13 March 1886
41 – Sheindel DOMENKOWICZ, daughter of Mendel Yitzhak, wife of Yeremyahu, 26 May 1917
42 – K? Leah, daughter of Yaakov, 14 August 1855
43 – Elimelech PRYNC, son of Yaakov, 18 May 1917
44 – Royza, daughter of Jakob TODRYSIAK, 7 January 1919
45 – Gitel Leah LIPSKI, daughter of Shlomo 19 April 1894
46 – Beila, daughter of Abraham, 16 October 1917
47 – Yitzhak, son of Shmuel, 21 October 1891
48 – Gitel, daughter of Matityahu, wife of Shlomo SZULC, 2 August 1905
49 – Yehuda Meir LIPSKI, son of Shlomo, 20 July 1898
50 – Gitel Leah, daughter of Idel HaKohen, wife of Abraham PRASZKER, 8 April 1924
51 – Abraham Yitzhak PANKIER, son of Shmuel, 20 May 1901
52 – Chava, daughter of Yaakov, 14 March 1886
53 – Ryvka Miryam, daughter of Akiva, 4 March 1907
54 – Beila, daughter of Shimon, 19 August 1904

55 – Baruch Shlomo? (KAC?), son of Yehuda HaKohen, spouse of Dvora Brana BIELAWSKI, 11 January 1892
56 – (no name)
57 – Freidel, daughter of Moshe Mordechai, 13 September 1885
58 – Tova Ester
59 – Ester Chai BIGELAJZEN, daughter of Shmuel Aharon, 12 June 1917
60 – Freida Necha JOZEFOWICZ, daughter of Michael Ze'ev JAKUBOWICZ, 29 April 1918
61 – Keila Elka, daughter of (Shlomo?) David (ASZ?), 8 April 1909
62 – Dvora Malka, daughter of Israel Chaim, 8 December 1910
63 – Chaim Baruch, son of Efraim Meir, 1 September 1908
64 – Hinda Ryvka, daughter of Shmay HaKohen, 16 April 1910
65 – Yehoshua Ze'ev LIDAUER, son of Israel, 27 March 1909
66 – Golda Leah BRZEZINSKI, daughter of Yosef Shlomo, 15 June 1915
67 – Yitzhak Yehuda, son of Abraham, 15 January 1912
68 – (no name, woman)
69 – Eliakum Getzel HOROWICZ, son of Moshe HaLevi, 26 November 1913
70 – Dvora, daughter of Zvi
71 – Yehuda, son of Ozer HaKohen, 2 September 1914
72 – Moshe David, son of Gabriel, 6 March 1894
73 – Yitzhak Yaakov, son of Abraham, 1 February 1895
74 – Sara Yuta, daughter of Eli, 3 December 1905
75 – Ayzik CWANG, son of Chaim, spouse of Rachel ZYMER, 29 August 1896
76 – Yeshayahu Ze'ev, son of Yosef Yaakov, 5 February 1908
77 – Chaya Malka, daughter of Efraim Fishel Cohen Tzedek, 8 November 1848
78 – Natan, son of Yeshayahu, 30 August 1873
79 – Aharon Yaakov, son of Benjamin, 29 April 1895
80 – Avigdor WIGDOROWICZ, son of Moshe HaKohen, spouse of Gitel Leah ZAURBACH, 17 November 1912
81 – Gitel Leah NOSAL, daughter of Moshe Aharon 12 November 1915
82 – Eliezer KOLSKI, son of Berek, spouse of Tana LAJZEROWICZ, 22 February 1913
83 – Freida, daughter of Abraham, 28 June 1865
84 – Chanyna Zelig, son of Hillel, 24 December 1868
85 – Chaya Roza, daughter of Yitzhak Ayzik, 8 June 1882
86 – ?, spouse of Abraham KOLSKI, 19 July 1894
87 – Shlomo, son of Yitzhak Ayzik, 26 July 1921
88 – Tova Sara SOSNOWSKI, daughter of Abraham HaKohen, 10 May 1915
89 – Shlomo, son of Eliakum Eliezer
90 – Asher, son of Mordechai HaLevi, 10 November 1902
91 – Moshe Chaim LICHTENSZTAJN, son of David, 11 May 1915
92 – (no name, woman)
93 – Zvi Hirsh KOZAK, son of Michael, spouse of Mindel KINCLER 19 December 1900
94 – Moshe, son of Yechezkel HaLevi, 17 August 1879
95 – Rachel Leah, daughter of Yitzhak KRAUER, 31 July 1873
96 – ?, HaKohen
97 – Yosef
98 – Henich, son of Shmuel Ze'ev, 20 September 1901
99 – Eliezer TORONCZYK
100 – Feiga SZWARC, wife of Aharon David, 20 May 1936
101 – Dyna ASZ, daughter of Efraim SOCHACZOWER, 2 November 1930
102 – Zvi, son of Moshe, 12 December 1877
103 – Abraham, son of Yitzhak, 17 July 1910
104 – Mirel, daughter of Yaakov, 19 April 1869
105 – Moshe, son of Shlomo, 24 April 1886
106 – Gela, daughter of David, 23 August 1852
107 – Ite Bracha FRENKEL, 1937
108 – Ester Sheina WINER
109 – Ester, daughter of Yehuda Leib, 3 July 1873

110 – Rechel Raca BRYL, daughter of Chaim BRYL, 5 January 1912
111 – Chana Liba ARBUS, daughter of Asher Anchel
112 – Eliezer
113 – Roza, daughter of Shimon, 29 June 1841
114 – Aharon, son of Michael, 30 November 1870
115 – Sara Rachel, daughter of Abraham Zvi, 8 May 1876
116 – Yosef Zvi, son of Abraham Yoel, 13 July 1924
117 – (no name), January or February 1916
118 – Golda
119 – Sara JAKUBOWICZ
120 – (no name)
121 – Gitel Reizel FUKS
122 – (no name, woman)
123 – Ester, daughter of Yaakov, 2 June 1902
124 – Chava Rojza ROZENBERG, daughter of Yaakov, 3 January 1923
125 – Nasha PASTERNAK, daughter of Ber Leib, 23 August 1928
126 – Adel WITKOWSKI, daughter of Mendel, 27 August 1923
127 – Beila BLAWAT, daughter of Reuven, 18 May 1911
128 – Bina JAKOBOWICZ
129 – Zvi Matityahu FRENKIEL, son of Shlomo, spouse of Liba GOLDMAN, 24 December 1926
130 – Yechiel Mabel GANSZER, son of Yehuda Leib, 28 March 1919
131 – (no name)
132 – ?, 18 January 1893
133 – Abraham Yitzhak GRINBAUM, son of Yehuda Leibush and Gitel Leah
134 – Tzipora Sime KORN, daughter of Yitzhak Meir PEREC, 5 March 1932
135 – Tane KOLSKI, daughter of Asher LAJZEROWICZ, wife of Leizer KOLSKI, 13 June 1918
136 – Tauba Sara BUGALSKI
137 – Chaya Leah RAK
138 – Leah, daughter of Shimon
139 – Yehoshua KRENIK, son of Yitzhak Yaakov, spouse of Perla WARSZAWSKI
140 – Ryvka, daughter of Shmuel, June or July 1928
141 – Pesa SZTARK
142 – (no name)
143 – Tzipora Perel, daughter of Abraham Aba HaLevi
144 – Liba FRENKIEL, daughter of Matityahu GOLDMAN, wife of Matys Hirsh, 20 May 1901
145 – Moshe Yaakov LAMANIC/LAMOWICZ, son of David Yehuda, 16 January 1896
146 – Foygel LUKS, daughter of Hersh GRDUK, wife of David Shlomo, 25 December 1906
147 – (no name, woman)
148 – Sheina EIDELMAN
149 – ? EISMANOWICZ, 18 December 1928
150 – Dora Glika, daughter of Moshe Zvi
151 – Sara Leah JACHIMOWICZ
152 – ?, daughter of Yitzhak Pinchas KAUBEC
153 – Elimelech HIRSZBAJN
154 – Abraham Yitzhak ZYSLING
155 – Liba TORONCZYK
156 – Rachel, daughter of Menachem
157 – ?, 1921 or 1922
158 – (no name, woman)
159 – ? FISZER

רשימת מצבות

55 – ברוך שלמה? (כץ?) בן יהודא הכהן, בעל דבורה בראנה ביעלאבסקי, י'א טבת תר'נב

56 – (?)

57 – פריידל בת משה מרדכי, ד' תשרי תר'מי

58 – תזבה אסתר

59 – אסתר חי ביגעלאייזען בת שמואל אהרון, כ'ב סיון תר'עז

60 – פריידא נעכא בת מיכל זאב, י'ז אייר תר'עח

61 – קיילא עלקא אש? בת שלמה? דוד, ב' דח"ה פסח תר'סט

62 – דבורה מלכה בת ישראל חיים, ז' כסליו תר'עא

63 – חיים ברוך בן אפרים מאיר, ה' אלול תר'סח

64 – הינדה רבקה בת שמעי הכהן, ז' ניסן תר'ע

65 – יהושע זאב בן ישראל לידאער, ה' ניסן תר'סט

66 – גאלדא לאה ברזעזינסקא בת יוסף שלמה, ג' תמוז תר'עה

67 – יצחק יהודה בן אברהם, כ'ה טבת תר'עב

68 – (?, אישה)

69 – אליקום געצל הורוויץ בן משה הלוי, כ'ו מרחשון תר'עד

70 – דבורה בת צבי

71 – יהודה בן עוזר, י'א אלול תר'עד

72 – משה דוד בן גבריאל, ר'ח אדר שני תר'נד

73 – יצחק יעקב בן אברהם, ז' שבט תר'נה

74 – שרה יוטא בת אלי, ה' כסליו תר'סו

75 – איציק צוואנג בן חיים, בעל רחל זימער, ר' אלול תר'נו

76 – ישעיהו זאב בן יוסף יעקב, ג' אדר ב' תר'סח

77 – חי מלכה בת אפרים פישל, י'ב מרחשון תר'ט

78 – נתן בן ישעיהו, ז' אלול תר"לג

79 – אהרון יעקב בן בנימין, ה' אייר תר'נה

80 – אביגדור וויגדאראווויץ בן משה, בעל גיטל לאה זאערבאך, ז' כסליו תר'עג

81 – גיטל לאה נאסעל בת משה אהרון, ה' כסליו תר'ו

82 – אליעזר קאלסקי בן דובער, בעל טאנה לייזראווויץ, ט'ו אדר ראשון תר'עג

83 – פריידא בת אברהם, ד' תמוז תר'כה

84 – חנינה זעליג בן הילל, י' טבת תר'כט

85 – חי' רוזה בת יצחק אייזיק, כ'א סיון תר'מב

86 – ? אשת אברהם קאלסקי, ט'ו אלול תר'נד

78 – שלמה בן יצחק אייזיק, כ' תמוז תר'פא

88 – טאבא שרה סאסנאווסקי בת אברהם, כ'ו אייר תר'עה

89 – שלמה בן אליקום אליעזר

90 – אשר בן מרדכי הלוי, י' חשון תר'סג

91 – משה חיים ליכטענשטיין בן דוד, כ"ז אייר תר'עה

92 – (?, אישה)

93 – צבי הירש בן מיכאל, ר'ז כסליו תר'סא

94 – משה בן יחזקאל הלוי, ר'ח מנחם אב תר'לט

95 – רחל לאה בת יצחק קראוער, ז' אב תר'לג

96 – ? הכהן

97 – יוסף

98 – העניך בן שמואל זאב, ז' תשרי תר'סב

99 – אליעזר טאראנטשיק

100 – פייגא שווארץ, אשת אהרון דוד, כ'ח אייר תר'צו

101 – דינה אש בת אפרים סאקאטשאווער, י'א חשון תר'צא

102 – צבי בן משה, ו' טבת תר'לח

103 – אברהם בן יצחק, י' תמוז תר'ע

104 – מירלה בת יעקב, ח' אייר תר'כט

105 – משה בן שלמה, ד' דח'וה'מ פסח תר'מו

106 – גאלא בת דוד, ח' אלול תר'יב

107 – יטע ברכה פרענקעל, תר'צז

108 – אסתר שיינא ווינער

109 – אסתר בת יהודא ליב, ח' תמוז תר'לג

110 – רעכל ראצא בת חיים, ט'ז טבת תר'עב

LIST OF ABBREVIATIONS

פ"נ	פה נקבר	Here is buried (at the beginning of the text, after a header)
תנצ"בה	תהי נפשו צרורה בצרור החיים	May her/his soul be bound up in the bonds of eternal life (at the end of the Hebrew text)
מו"ה	מורנו הרב	our teacher the rav (followed by name)
לפ"ק	לפרט קטן	(follows a date, indicates the year does not include the thousands, usually the "5000")
ר"	רב	reb (honorific for a man)
ב"ר	בן/בת רֶב	son/daughter of reb (followed by name of father)
נ"י	נרו יאיר	may his light shine ("i.e. may he live a long life", indicates the person mentioned was alive, usually a relative of the deceased)
ז"ל	זכרונו/ה לברכה	of blessed memory (after the name of a deceased person)
מו"ר	מורנו ורבנו	our teacher and rabbi
נפ"	נפטר	passed away
אב"ד	אב בית דין	president/head of rabbinical tribunal
[ב]ר"ח	[ב]ראש חודש	[on] the first day of the month (in the Jewish calendar)
בש"ט	בשם טוב	in a good name (usually after "passed away")

ציון קבר	Grave monument

מה רב השבר יזעק כל גבר	How great a woe all men will cry out!
רבתי בנשים הובלה לקבר	My love among women was taken to the grave.
יראת השם צנועה וחסידה	God-fearing, modest and righteous,
מאד יקרה במבחר שנות'	very dear, cut down at her best years,
מ' **מרים ריבקה** בת מוה"	Mrs. **Miryam Ryvka**, daughter of our teacher the rav
חיים יהודה ז"ל נפטרה	**Chaim Yehuda**, of blessed memory, passed away
בר"ח שבט שנ' תר'סט	on the 23rd of January 1909.
לפ'ק ת'נ'צ"ב'ה'	May her soul be bound up in the bonds of eternal life.

2 – Ester (ZAURBACH?), daughter of Yeshayahu (GUTMAN?)

אשה מהוללה ורכה בשנים	A highly praised young woman
סחרה במעשים טובים ונאמנים	dealt in good and trustworthy deeds
תמיד גומלת חסדים היתה	she always rendered charity
רשות מפעלה מלפנים לקחה	with authority she put her project ahead
בכל דרכיה הלכה ביושר	in all her deeds she dealt honestly
ת__ אשר מעשי(ה) בכושר	all her activities were capably done.
ידיה פרשה להפושט יד	She stretched her hands to the needy
שמה בטחונה בהפותח יד	she put her trust in the generous.
עתה הלכה לעולמה התחי'	Now she had passed away,
יהללוה וישבחוה על מעשי'	she will be praised and lauded for all her deeds
המון אנשים מכירים ויודעים	masses of people are acquainted and know
ויאמרו מנוחתה מבורך ונעים	and will bless her resting in comfort.
ה"ה מרת **אסתר** בת **ישעי** ז"ל	Mrs. **Ester**, daughter of **Yeshayahu**, of blessed memory

3 – Sara, daughter of Moshe HaKohen, 3 March 1887

עלמה יקרה	Dear maiden
הבתולה **שרה** בת	the virgin **Sara**, daughter of
ר' **משה** הכהן נ"י	Mr. **Moshe** HaKohen, may his light shine,
נ' ט' ז' אדר ראשון	died 3rd of March
תר'מז תנצ"בה	1887. May her soul be bound up in the bonds of eternal life.

חיים יוסף	**Chaim Yosef**
מרקוס	**Markus**

פ"נ מוה **חיים יוסף** ב"ר	Here is buried our teacher the rav **Chaim Yosef**, son of
משה ז"ל נפ' כ'ה חשוון	**Moshe**, of blessed memory, passed away on the 10th of
שנת תר'עח לפ'ק	November on the year 1917.
ת'נ'צ'ב'ה'	May his soul be bound up in the bonds of eternal life.

פ'נ מצבת קבורת אשת חיל
רבת מעללים רדפה צדקה
וחסד מנעוריה אהבה תורה
ויראת ה' הרבנית הצדיקת
מ' **פריווא** בת הרבנו המופלג
החריף השנון מו"ר **חיים** ז"ל
ואשת הגאון הגדול אדמו"ר
הרב ר' **ישראל יהושע** אב"ד
דפה זצו"קל בעל המחבר
ספר ישועות ישראל
נפטרה בש"ט י'ט חשון
ש' תר'ס לפ'ק
תנצב"ה

The burial headstone of a valiant woman
with many good deeds. Since her childhood pursued charity
and kindness, she loved the Torah
and feared God, the sainted rabitzen
Mrs. **Prywe**, daughter of our eminent Rabbi, learned and
erudite, our teacher Rav **Chaim**, of blessed memory,
and wife of the great genius, our master and teacher, *Admor*
the rabbi reb **Israel Yehoshua**, a Head Judge,
___ saintly and holy of blessed memory, writer
of the book "*The Salvations of Israel*".
Passed away in a good name on the 23rd of October
of the year1899.
May her soul be bound up in the bonds of eternal life.

6 – Yaakov MOSZKOWICZ, son of Mordechai HaLevi

Here is buried reb **Yaakov Moszkowicz**   פ'נ ר' **יעקב מאשקאוויץ**

Here is buried an innocent and upright man   פ'נ איש תם וישר
_____ wise honorable and happy   ___ חכם נכבד ומאושר
our teacher the reb **Yaakov**, son of our teacher the rav   מוה" **יעקב** בן מוה" רב
Mordechai HaLevi, of blessed memory, passed away on   **מרדכי** הלוי ז"ל נפטר
11th of Elul on the year ____.   י'א אלול שנת תר__
May his soul be bound up in the bonds of eternal life.   ת'נ'צ'ב'ה'

7 – Baruch Shlomo BOK, son of Abraham Yitzhak, 29 December 1915

אהה על השבר	Woe for a heartbreak
כי הובל לקבר	because was taken to his grave
הבחור המפואר כמ'	the splendid young man as
ברוך שלמה בן מוה'	**Baruch Shlomo**, son of our teacher the rav
אברהם יצחק באק נ'	**Abraham Yitzhak Bok**, may his light shine,
נפ' כ'ב. טבת תר'עו לפ'ק	passed away 29th of December 1915.

הערשקאוויטש _____ מ' _____ Mrs. _____ **Herszkowicz**

אסתר אסאסקא   **Ester Ososka**

נפטרה ביום י'א מרחשון
שנת תר"סה לפ'ק

---

passed away on the 20th of October,
on the year 1904.

פנחס ברוך ווארצעל	Pinchas Baruch Worcel
פ נ	Here is buried
אבינו היקר והתמים	Our dear upright father
ר' פנחס ברוך	reb **Pinchas Baruch**
ב'ר בן ציון ז"ל	son of **Ben Zion**, of blessed memory,
נ'פ ביום י'ב אב	passed away on 30th of July
שנת תר'סט	of the year 1909.

11 – Moshe, son of Eliezer, 1905-1906

מר _____ Mr. _____
שבת בדרך התורה _____ in the way of the Torah
הה על____ת ד' הטהורה The very one _____ the pure.
אבינו ____ **משה** בן Our father ___ **Moshe,** son of
ל_____ **אליעזר** ז"ל ___ **Eliezer,** of blessed memory,
י_____ תר'סו לפק passed away in (1905-1906)
תנ'צבה May his soul be bound up in the bonds of eternal life.

12 – Sheina, daughter of Shraga, 6 June 1907

אהה	Woe
על השבר שקראנו	for the calamity that befell us
שנלקח בתנו היקרה	that our darling daughter was taken from us
מ' **שיינא** בת **שרגא**	Ms. **Sheina**, daughter of **Shraga**,
נ"י נפטרה כ'ד סיון	may his light shine, passed away 6th of June
שנת	on the year
תר'סז לפ'ק ת'נ'צ'ב'ה'	1907. May her soul be bound up in the bonds of eternal life.

פ'נ ר' **שמואל שלמה** ב"ר **משה**
סג"ל

Here is buried reb **Shmuel Shlomo**, son of reb **Moshe**
HaLevi (Segal)

ושמואל שב למקום מחצבתו
שם שם לו מקום מנוחתו
לב טוב ואיש ישר ותמים

And **Shmuel** returned to the place of his origin
where he made a place for his rest.
A good hearted, honest and fair man,

14 – Moshe Aharon, son of Yitzhak, 29 April 1903

הבן הישר ___	___ the dear son
___תה שמים	____ sky
נישמתו תהי בצרור החיים	his soul will be in the bonds of eternal life.
מו' **משה אהרון** ב'ר **יצחק**	Our teacher **Moshe Aharon**, son of reb **Yitzhak**,
נ'פ. ב' אייר תו"סג תנצ"בה	passed away on the 29th of April 1903. May his soul be bound up in the bonds of eternal life.

15 – Chaya Dvora, daughter of Pinchas Zelig, 18 May 1901

פ'נ האישה החשובה
והצנועה רכה בשנים
יראת ה' מרת **חיה דבורה**
בת מוה" **פנחס זעליג**
נ"י נפ' בערב ר"ח סיון

שנ' תר'סא לפ'ק תנצב"ה

Here is buried the important woman
the modest, of tender years,
God-fearing, Mrs. **Chaya Dvora**
daughter of our teacher the rav **Pinchas Zelig**,
may his light shine, passed away on the eve
of the 19th of May
1901. May her soul be bound up in the bonds of eternal life.

16 – Mordechai, son of Moshe Aharon, 29 May 1901

פ' נ'	Here is buried
מר לנו על גורל השבר	We are bitter for the heart-breaking fate
כי גז חיש הובל לקבר	because quickly he passed and was taken to the grave
בחור מפואר ורגיג באורייתא	A splendid young man and well versed in the Bible
במקרא במשנה ובריתא	the Mishna and its extraneous teachings
כמר **מרדכי** בן מו'הרב	as Mr. **Mordechai**, son of our teacher the rav
משה אהרן נ"י נפטר	**Moshe Aharon**, may his light shine, passed away
י'א סיון שנ' תר'כא לפק	29th of May 1901
ת נ צ ב"ה	May his soul be bound up in the bonds of eternal life.

17 – Eliezer MANES, son of Menachem, 14 May 1885

איש אמונים	A trustworthy man
הלך כל ימיו בדרך	throughout his life he followed the way
הישר הישיש הנכבד	of righteousness, the honorable old man.
החבר ר' **אליעזר**	Comrade reb **Eliezer**,
בן החבר ר' **מנחם** ז"ל	son of comrade reb **Menachem**, of blessed memory,
נפטר ביום ו' עש'ק	passed away on Friday, eve of the Holy Shabbat
ר'ח סיון שנת תר'מה	14th of May of the year 1885.
תנצ'בה	May his soul be bound up in the bonds of eternal life.

18 – Sheindel

פ נ	Here is buried
שמים עלתה למקומה	She went up to her place in heaven,
ידיה תמכו לדלים מסכנים	supported the poor and wretched,
ישרכ ישרת לב וצנועה במעשיה	Righteous and modest in her deeds
נו ה _____	_____
דאבון לב עזבה בקרבנו	She left us a heartache.
לקבר הובל מחמד עינינו	To the grave was the apple of our eyes taken
האישה הכשרה והיקרה	the dear honest woman
מרת **שיינדל**	Mrs. **Sheindel**

19 – Gitel ARONOWICZ, daughter of Israel, 17 November 1913

פ' נ'	Here is buried
מ' גיטל אראנאוויץ	Mrs. **Gitel Aronowicz**
───────────	───────────
אשת חיל צנועה וכשרה	A woman of valor, modest and proper,
יראת ה' היא תתהלל	God-fearing and praised.
מ' **גיטל** בת	Mrs. **Gitel**, daughter of
ר' **ישראל** ז"ל נפטרה	reb **Israel**, of blessed memory, passed away
י'ז מרחשון בשנת	on the 17th of November of the year
תר'עד תנצב"ה	1913. May her soul be bound up in the bonds of eternal life.

20 – Aharon, son of Yosef 12 April 1899

אבינו היקר	Our dear father,
איש נכבד ומאושר	a happy, honorable man,
אהב מעודו דרך הישר	always loved the righteous ways.
הה'ר **אהרן** בן	Reb **Aharon**, son of
הה'ר **יוסף** נפטר ביום	reb **Yosef**, passed away on day
ב' אייר תר'נט לפ'ק	12th of April 1899.
תנצ"בה	May his soul be bound up in the bonds of eternal life.

21 – Ahuva (Liba?) FRENKIEL?, daughter of Matityahu GOLDMAN, spouse of Matys Hersh?, 8 August 1909

נ'י _____ פ נ   Here lies _____, may his light shine.

אהה על השבר כי   Woe for the calamity that
הובלה לקבר אשה   the woman carried to the grave

_____ ו   _____
_____ ב   _____
_____ ה   _____ daughter of

מטיהו נ'י גאלדמאן   **Matityahu Goldman**, may his light shine,
נפ' כ'א מנחם אב שנת   passed away 8th of August on the year
תר'סט לפ'ק תנצב"ה   1909. May her soul be bound up in the bonds of eternal life.

פנחס זאב ב'ר	**Pinchas Ze'ev** son of reb
יהודה ז"ל נפטר י"ד	**Yehuda**, of blessed memory, passed away the 15th
ימים לחודש אלול	day of the month of September,
שנת תר'נד לפ'ק	on the year 1894.
ת'נ'צ'ב'ה'	May his soul be bound up in the bonds of eternal life.

23 – Bracha, daughter of Yehoshua Ayzik, 27 May 1870

פ 'נ'	Here is buried
האישה הזקנה	The old woman,
ברכה בת כר __	Mrs. **Bracha**, daughter of __
יהושע איזק ז"ל	**Yehoshua Ayzik**, of blessed memory,
מתה כ'ו אייר תר'ל	died 27th of May 1870.
לפ'ק ת'נ'צ'ב'ה'	May her soul be bound up in the bonds of eternal life.

24 – Menachem Yehuda FALC, son of Naftali Zvi, 8 April 1916

מנחם	**Menachem**
יהודא	**Yehuda**
פאלץ	**Falc**

פ"נ מוה" **מנחם יהודא** ז"ל — Here is buried our teacher the rav **Menachem Yehuda**, of blessed memory,

ב"ר **נפתלי צבי** נ"י — son of **Naftali Zvi**, may his light shine,

נפ' ה' ניסן שנת תר'עו לפ'ק — passed away on the 8th of April 1916.

פה ינוח איש צעיר לימים — Resting here is a young man

בכל שנותיו הלך תמים — who followed the righteous ways all his life

זקן ושבע ימים ____	Old man and full of years ____,
ב"ר **יעקב** הלוי נפ __ 'טבת	son of **Yaakov** HaLevi, passed away ____ of (December-January)
שנ' תר'עח תנצב"ה	on the year (1917-1918). May his soul be bound up in the bonds of eternal life.

26 – Sara, daughter of Moshe Dov HaKohen, 30 June 1904

אשה נכבדה _____	An honorable woman
אוהבת דרך ישרה	Loves the righteous way of life
מ' **שרה** בת	Mrs. **Sara** daughter of
ר' **משה דב** הכהן	reb **Moshe Dov** HaKohen,
נפטרה י'ז תמוז	passed away on the 30th of June
ש' תר'סד	of the year 1904.

27 – Eliezer KLINGBAJL, son of Chaim, 14 May 1892

פ"נ מו'ר **אליעזר** בן מו'ר **חיים** ז"ל נ'
בש"ט י'ז אייר תר'נב לפ'ק

אהה יגון קרנו מות אבינו
לאבל נהפך פתאום מחולינו
ישר ותמים הה אבד מאתנו
עובד ד' כל הימים
זרע צדקות על כל מים
ר_____לב יראי שמים
איש תבת_ _הגה ב_נורה הה
הרבנו המופלג מו'ר **אליעזר**
בהרבנו המופלג מו'ר **חיים** ז"ל
תנצ"בה

Here is buried our teacher Mr. **Eliezer**, son of our teacher Mr. **Chaim**, of blessed memory, passed away in a good name on the 14th of May 1892.
Woe, sorrow befell us on our father's death!
Our joy was suddenly changed into mourning.
Honest and fair. He was lost to us.
He followed God's law all his days,
spread charity everywhere.
_____ heart, God-fearing,
a man _____ the very one,
Our eminent Rabbi, our teacher, **Eliezer**
son of our eminent Rabbi, our teacher **Chaim**, of blessed memory.
May his soul be bound up in the bonds of eternal life.

פ'נ	Here is buried
אהה עלי גורל השבר	Woe for a heart-breaking fate,
נקטף באבו והובל לקבר	cut down in his youth and brought to the grave.
שבר מר ואבל אך לנו	We have only bitter heartbreak and mourning;
לקבר הובל נזר ראשנו	our head's crown was taken to the grave,
הבחור **אנשל** בן מו"ה	the young man **Anshel**, son of our teacher
צבי ליב ביבערגאל נפט'	**Zvi Leib Bibergal**, passed away
יו'ד תמוז תר'עו תנצב"ה	on the 5th of July 1916. May his soul be bound up in the bonds of eternal life.

29 – Israel, son of Eli HaKohen, 18 March 1896

ספדו מר על השבר	Mourn bitterly for the heartbreak
במות פתאם זה הגבר	caused by the sudden death of this man
בעודו היה איש צעיר	while still a young man.
הה! יתומים קטנים השאיר	Alas! Small orphans he left
כה **ישראל** ב'ר **אלי**' הכהן	here. **Israel**, son of **Eli** HaKohen,
נפטר ד' ניסן תר'נו לפ'ק	passed away on the 18th of March 1896.
תנצ"בה	May his soul be bound up in the bonds of eternal life.

פ"נ	Here is buried
אשה חשובה	An important woman,
רכה בשנים יראת ה'	young, God-fearing,
היא תתהלל מרת	she is praised. Mrs.
חנה קרעניק	**Chana Krenik**,
בת מוה" עקיבה ז"ל	daughter of our teacher the rav **Akiva**, of blessed memory,
ת'נ'צ' ב 'ה'	May her soul be bound up in the bonds of eternal life.

_____י נחמד חמדת הוריו הילד
ישראל מאיר בן מוה' אברהם נ'י
נפטר ך'ב אדר תר'ן לפ'ק
ישר וזך ילד רך
אל בית הספר צעד ופרח
מהיות בחלד עול ימים
אליו קראה מן השמים
יללו הוריו על הלקח
ראש מחמדיהם בל ישראל

_____ lovely, the delight of his parents. The boy
Israel Meir, son of our teacher the rav **Abraham**, may his light shine,
passed away on the 14th of March 1890.
A young boy honest and pure
adolescent boy going to school
In his lifetime he was just a youngster
when called from the sky.
His parents wailed that taken from them
was their most beloved **Israel**

32 – Yehuda, son of Moshe, 18 November 1912

_____ יהודה ב"ר משה ז"ל
נפטר יום ב' ח' כסליו בשנת
תר'עג לפ'ק תנצבה"

אל מלא רחמים שוכן במרומים
המצא מנוחה נכונה על כנפי
השכינה
במעלות קדושים וטהורים כוכבים
ברקיע מזהירים את נשמת
_____ ב"ר משה _____

_____ **Yehuda**, son of **Moshe**, of blessed memory,
passed away on Monday the 18th of November
1912. May his soul be bound up in the bonds of eternal life.

Merciful God, who resides in the heavens,
on divine wings bring a true rest

in the heights where the holy and the pure, stars
in the sky brightens the soul of
_____ son of reb **Moshe** _____

33 – (no name, man)

פנ'	Here is buried
איש ירא אלקים	A God-fearing man
וסר מרע כל ימים	and turned away from evil all his days
מעשיו היו ביושר	His actions were done in fairness

הה' מוה' **ברוך יצחק**	our teacher the rav **Baruch Yitzhak**
ב'ר **אפרים ראזענצווייג**	son of reb **Efraim Rozencwajg**,
נפטר ב ש'ט ג' כסליו	passed away in a good name, on the 19th of November
תר'מח לפק	in the year 1887.
תנצ"בה	May his soul be bound up in the bonds of eternal life.

35 – Gershon, son of Yaakov, 5 September 1896

פ"נ	Here is buried
ספדו על זה הגבר	Mourn this man
כי פתאם הובל לקבר	for suddenly he was taken to the grave.
איש נכבד ומאושר	An honored, happy man,
הלך בדרך הישר הח'ר	followed the righteous way. Our sage Rabbi
גרשון בן הח'ר **יעקב**	**Gershon**, son of the sage Rabbi **Yaakov**,
נפטר ך"ז אלול תר'נו לפ'ק	passed away on the 5th of September 1896.
תנצ'בה	May his soul be bound up in the bonds of eternal life.

36 – Sara, daughter of Abraham, 25 January 1912

נקטפו ימיה _____ _____ her days were cut short.
אהה באבה רחקה מבניה Woe! While young she was taken away from her sons.
מ' **שרה** בת מוה' **אברהם** Mrs. **Sara**, daughter of our teacher the rav **Abraham**,
ז"ל נפטרה ו' שבט שנ' of blessed memory, passed away on the 25th of January
תר'עב לפ'ק תנצב"ה 1912. May her soul be bound up in the bonds of eternal life.

37 – Nesha, daughter of Gershon

מ' **נעשא** בת   Mrs. **Nesha**, daughter of
__ **גרשון** ז"ל   __ **Gershon**, of blessed memory.

פה תנוח האישה היקרה   Here rests the dear woman.
אשת חיל צנוע ובש__   A woman of valor, modest and ____,
יראת השם נפש טהורה   God-fearing pure soul,
לעניים תמכה ידיה   from her hand she supported the poor

38 – Yehuda, son of Yaakov, 26 December 1910

Man is like a vapor	אדם להבל דמה
His days are a passing shadow	ימיו כצל עובר

Here is buried an honest and righteous man,	פ"נ איש תם וישר
God-fearing, our teacher the rav **Yehuda**,	ירא ה' מוה" **יהודא**
son of reb **Yaakov** of blessed memory, passed away	בן ר' **יעקב** ז"ל נפטר
on the first of Chanuka, the 26th of December 1910.	א' דחנוכה תר'עא
May his soul be bound up in the bonds of eternal life.	לפ'ק ת'נ'צ'ב'ה'

39 – Tauba Keila (BROD?), daughter of Moshe (MAUER?), 28 January 1871

טובת פעלים רבת מעללים	Of many and good deeds
ורב כשרון מעשים כולם מהללים	and much practical talent — all are praising.
יד עני ואביונו קרובים	The hands of the poor and the needy she held close,
בכל כוחה החזיקה בידיה	with all her strength she held them in her hand.
אהה אומללה אשה כשירה במעשיה	Woe, wretched is the woman proper in her deeds.
~~	~~~~~~~~~~~~~~~
קינה ונהו בלבנו עלי מותה	Lament and wailings in our hearts for her death.
יום ש'ק ו' שבט תר'לא שבה למנוחתה	On Holy Shabbat 28th January 1871, she returned to her rest.
יראת ד' תמימה וישרה היתה	God-fearing, pure and honest she was,
לטוב זכרוה חכמת נשים	remember her with kindness wise women.
אם היתה לדלים ורשים	She was a mother to the needy and the poor.

40 – Beila, daughter of Moshe, 13 March 1886

פ' נ'   Here is buried

מה גדול הבכי בעיר   Great is the cry in the town
אל מות זאת האישה   on the death of this woman
הצעירה נכבדה ויראת   young, respected and God-fearing.
ד' מרת **ביילא** בת   Mrs. **Beila**, daughter of
החבר ר' **משה** ז"ל   the comrade reb **Moshe**, of blessed memory,
נ' בש'ק ו' אדר שני   passed away on Holy Shabbat, 13th of March
שנת תר'מו לפק   of the year 1886.
תנצ"בה   May her soul be bound up in the bonds of eternal life.

41 – Sheindel DOMENKOWICZ, daughter of Mendel Yitzhak, wife of Yermyahu, 29 May 1917

פ' נ'	Here is buried
מ' **שיינדל** בת ר' **מענדל יצחק** נ'י	Mrs. **Sheindel**, daughter of the rabbi **Mendel Yitzhak**, may his light shine,
אשת ר' **יריהי'**	wife of reb **Yermyahu**
דאמענקאוויטש	**Domenkowicz**,
ער"ח סיון ש' תר'עז	29th of May of the year 1917.
שב _____	_____
ייללו ב _____	And they wailed in the _____
נגדע אנה _____	was cut off _____
ד" ל ____	God _____
לאור שם באור החיים	And will be lit there by the life-light.
ת נ צ ב ה	May her soul be bound up in the bonds of eternal life.

42 – K? Leah, daughter of Yaakov, 14 August 1855

הוז___ כן	_____
הה האישה הצנועה	Woe, the modest woman
הייקרה והכשרה מר'	the dear and proper Mrs.
ק___ לאה	**K_____ Leah**
בת הנגיד ___ה' **יאקב** נ'י	daughter of the leader our teacher reb **Yaakov**, may his light shine,
נונ **ב**_____ נפטרה ביום ג	descendant of **B**_____ passed away on Tuesday
א' דר'ח אלול תרטו לפ'ק	14th of August 1855.
תנצבה	May her soul be bound up in the bonds of eternal life.

עין משפט ____ _____

פ"נ איש תם וישר ירא ה'
ורדף אך במצות ביקור חולים
ולוית המת. והיה אחד מחברה
קדושה רפה מוה" **אלימלך** בן
מוה" **יעקב** ז"ל **פרינץ**. נפטר יום

כ'ו אייר שנת תר'עז לפ'ק

Here is buried an upright and honest man, God-fearing
and pursues the commandments to attend the sick,
to take part in funeral processions, and was a member of the
burial society _____. Our teacher the rav **Elimelech**, son of
our teacher the rav **Yaakov Prync**, of blessed memory,
passed away
on the 18th of May 1917.

44 – Royza, daughter of Yaakov TODRYSIAK, 7 January 1919

רויזא	**Royza**,
ב'ר יעקב טאדרישאק	daughter of reb **Yaakov Todrysiak**,
נפ' ו' שבט תר'עט	passed away on the 7th of January 1919.
תנצ"בה	May her soul be bound up in the bonds of eternal life.

45 – Gitel Leah LIPSKI, daughter of Shlomo, 19 April 1894

פ'ט האשה **גיטל לאה** ב'ר **שלמה**
ליפסקי ז"ל
נפטרה י'ג ניסן תרנד

Here is buried the woman **Gitel Leah**, daughter of reb
Shlomo Lipski, of blessed memory,
passed away 19th of April 1894

האשה
גיטל לאה פה קבורה
נשמתה בצרור החיים צרורה
יום זכר כבתה נרה
בירח זיו מתה היקרה
טהורה בחיים נהי נקצרה
ובא השמש ונטל הדרה
לבעלה הרחיבה דעתה באוצרה
אשה נאה כלים ודירה
לאה כרות רבקה ושרה
יראת ה' ואהבת התורה
אביונים ועניים חזקה בצרה
בורא העולם הוא מכירה
הדלת פסחה לזעק מרה
עלתה רומה לקבל שכרה
גיטל לאה ליפסקי כמנורה
_____ בשמן הטהורה

The woman
Gitel Leah is buried here,
    her soul is bound up in the bonds of eternal life.
the day for remembering her candle was sniffed
    ____ lustre. The dear had died
Pure in life wailing was cut short
    The sun had come and took away her beauty.
She had an open mind towards her husband. In her treasury,
    the pretty woman, and apartment and utensils
Leah like Ruth, Rebecca and Sara.
    Feared God and loved the Torah.
She strengthens the poor and the needy when in trouble.
    The world creator knows her.
She passed the door to cry out bitterly
    She went proudly to receive her due
Gitel Leah Lipski like a lamp
    _____ in pure oil.

46 – Bila, daughter of Abraham, 16 October 1917

פה תנוח אשה יקרה	Here rests a dear woman
אשת חיל צנועה וכשרה	a woman of valor, modest and proper.
צדקה פזרה כל ימי חייה	All through her life she dispersed charity,
מכניסה אורחים כל ימיה	was hospitable always.
מרת **בילה** בת מוה'	Mrs. **Bila**, daughter of our teacher the rav
אברהם ז"ל נפטרה בת __	**Abraham**, of blessed memory, passed away at age __
שנים יום א' דר"ח חשוון	on the 17th of October
שנת תר'עח לפ'ק	on the year 1917.
ת'נ'צ'ב'ה'	May her soul be bound up in the bonds of eternal life.

אשר הגה בתורה ו_ אד
מו'ר **יצחק** בן מו'ר **שמואל**
נפטר ד' דחוהמוס" תר'נב לפ'ק
בכינו הה גוע ואיננו
נקטף ילדיו רבים עודנו
שם שומעי השבר
שומר מצות מעודו זה הגבר
בחלוניו עלה פרץ פרץ
בעזרת בניו השליך ארץ

that studied the Torah and ___
our teacher reb **Yitzhak** son of our teacher reb **Shmuel**
passed away on the 21nd of October 1891.
We cried woe, he died and is no more
___ was cut down, his children are many still is
there who heard of the catastrophe
He followed the commandments always, this man.
his windows were broken through
With the help of his sons he threw down

———————   ———————

48 – Gitel, daughter of Matityahu, wife of Shlomo SZULC, 2 August 1905

במעשי ההיתה ישרה	She was honest in all her deeds,
עשתה צדקה וחסד. מ'	she gave kindness and charity. Mrs.
גיטל בת ר' **מתתי** ז"ל	**Gitel**, daughter of reb **Matityahu**, of blessed memory,
אר' **שלמה שולטץ** נ"י	wife of reb **Shlomo Szulc**, may his light shine,
נפטרה בש'ט ביום	passed away in a good name, on day
ד' ר'ח מנחם אב	2nd of August
ש' תר'סה לפ'ק	of the year 1905
תנצ"בה	May her soul be bound up in the bonds of eternal life.

אִישׁ זה למד תורה דעה
ותבונה הרבנו המופלג
החסיד מו'ר **יהודא מאיר**
בן ה'ה מו'ה **שלמה** ז"ל
נפטר ר'ח אב ש' תר'נח לפ'ק

תנצ"בה

This man studied the Torah, knowledge
and reason. Our distinguished scholar Rabbi,
the righteous, our teacher reb **Yehuda Meir**
son of our teacher the rav **Shlomo**, of blessed memory,
passed away on the 20th of July 1898.

May his soul be bound up in the bonds of eternal life.

פ"נ	Here is buried
אמנו היקרה וחשובה	Our dear and important mother
גיטל לאה	**Gitel Leah**,
ב"ר **ידעל** הכהן	daughter of reb **Idel** HaKohen,
אשת ר' **אברהם**	wife of reb **Abraham**
פראשקער	**Praszker**,
נפ' ד' ניסן תר'פד	passed away on the 8th of April, the year 1924.
ת נ צ ב ה	May her soul be bound up in the bonds of eternal life.

51 – Abraham Yitzhak PANKIER, son of Shmuel, 20 May 1901

גבר יהיה	A man will be
_אה מות	_____ death

פ"נ איש ישר הלך בדרך	Here is buried a man, honest and
תמים מוה" **אברהם יצחק**	upright. Our teacher the rav **Abraham Yitzhak**
בן מוה" **שמואל** ז"ל נפט'	son of our teacher the rav **Shmuel**, of blessed memory, passed away
ב' סיון שנת תר"סא לפ'ק	on the 20th of May, on the year 1901.
ת' נ' צ' ב' ה'	May his soul be bound up in the bonds of eternal life.

52 – Chava, daughter of Yaakov, 14 March 1886

פ' נ'	Here is buried
אמנו היקרה	Our dear mother,
אשה נכבדה וישרה	an honorable and honest woman,
הצנועה יראת ה'	the modest, God-fearing,
מ' **חוה** בת הח'ר **יאקב**	Mrs. **Chava**, daughter of the sage reb **Yaakov**,
נ' ז' אדר שני תר"מו	passed away on the 14th of March, the year 1886.
תנצ"בה	May her soul be bound up in the bonds of eternal life.

53 – Ryvka Miryam, daughter of Akiva, 4 March 1907

מהוללה היתה _____ — She was praised _____
בדרך התורה הדריכה ___ — She guided ____ in the laws of the Torah.
מ' **רבקה מרים** בת — Mrs. **Ryvka Miryam**, daughter of the
הה מוה' **עקיבא** ז"ל — very one, our teacher the Rabbi **Akiva**, of blessed memory,
נפ' י"ח אדר ש' תר"סז לפ'ק — passed away on the 4th of March, on the year 1907.
תנצ"בה — May her soul be bound up in the bonds of eternal life.

54 – Beila, daughter of Shimon, 19 August 1904

_____ורה

מ' **ביילא** בת ר' **שמעון** ז'ל

נפטרה יום ח' אלול ונקברה

י' אלול תר"סד לפ'ק תנצ"בה

_____ and pure

Mrs. **Beila**, daughter of **Shimon**, of blessed memory, passed away on the 19th of August, and was buried on the 21st of August 1904. May her soul be bound up in the bonds of eternal life.

55 – Baruch Shlomo KAC, son of Yehuda, spouse of Dvora Brane BIELAWSKA, 11 January 1892

פ נ	Here lies
איש הישר ____	A righteous man ____
תמים במעשיו ____	who was fair in what he did.
נהנה מיגיע כפיו ה__ __	He enjoyed the fruits of his labor.
ברוך שלמה בן _____	**Baruch Shlomo**, son of _____
יהודא כץ _____	**Yehuda Kac** ____

57 – Freidel, daughter of Moshe Mordechai, 13 September 1885

פ' נ'	Here is buried
אשה זקנה	An old woman,
הצנועה מ' **פריידל**	the modest Mrs. **Freidel**,
בת הח'ר **משה מרדכי**	daughter of the learned reb **Moshe Mordechai**,
נפטרה ד' תשרי	passed away on the 13th of September
שנת תר'מו לפ'ק	on the year 1885.
תנצ"בה	May her soul be bound up in the bonds of eternal life.

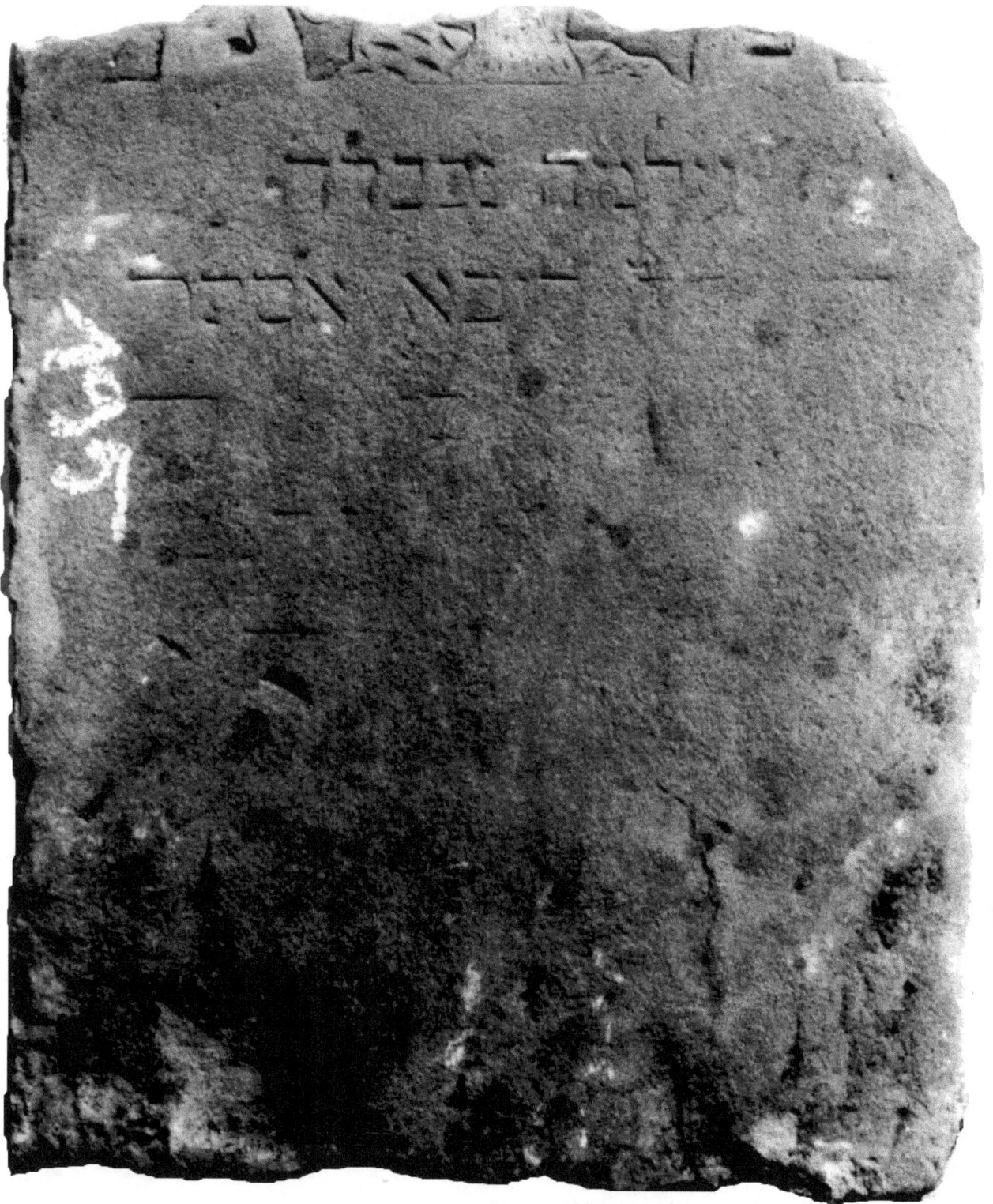

		maiden buried	עלמה נכבדה _____
		Tova Ester	**תובא אסתר** _____

אסתר חי ביגעלאייזען	**Ester Chai Bigelajzen**
פ נ	Here lies
————	
ד' את נשמתה יסתירה	God (took?) her _____ soul.
אסתר חי'	**Ester Chai**,
ב'ר **שמואל אהרון**	daughter of reb **Shmuel Aharon**,
נפ. כ"ב סיון תר'עז	passed away on the 12th of June 1917.
ת נ צ ב ה	May her soul be bound up in the bonds of eternal life.

60 – Freida Necha JOZEFOWICZ, daughter of Michal Ze'ev JAKUBOWICZ, wife of Enoch, 29 April 1918

פ"נ	Here is buried
האישה הכשרה יראת ה'	The worthy, God-fearing woman,
רכה בשנים, טובת לב. מ'	young, good hearted, Mrs.
פרידא נעכא	**Freida Necha**
יוזעפאוויטש	**Jozefowicz**
בת **מיכל זאב** נ"י	daughter of **Michal Ze'ev**, may his light shine,
נפטרה	passed away
י"ז לחודש אייר שנ'	the 29th of the month of April, on the year
תר"עח לפ'ק	1918
ת'נ'צ'ב'ה'	May her soul be bound up in the bonds of eternal life.

61 – Keila Elka, daughter of Shlomo David ASZ, 8 April 1909

פ'נ אשה חשובה וישרה
במצותי היתה נזהרה
יראת ה' צנועה וכשרה
הה! בלי בנים נעדרה
מ' **קיילא עלקא** ב"ר
שלמה דוד ז'ל נפ' ב' דח"ה
פסח, שנת תר'סט לפ'ק תנצבה

Here is buried an important and honest woman.
She was careful in following my commandments
God-fearing, modest and proper,
alas! without sons. Missing is
Mrs. **Keila Elka**, daughter of reb
Shlomo David, of blessed memory, passed away on the 8th
of April 1909. May her soul be bound up in the bonds of
eternal life.

62 – Dvora Malka, daughter of Israel Chaim, 8 December 1910

פ'נ אישה	Here is buried a woman
חשובה וצנועה	important and modest,
יראת ה' היא תתהלל	God-fearing. She will be praised.
מ' **דבורה מלכה** בת	Mrs. **Dvora Malka**, daughter of
ר' **ישראל חיים** ז"ל	reb **Israel Chaim**, of blessed memory,
נפ' ז' כסליו שנת	passed away on the 8th of December of the year
תר'עא לפ'ק תנ'צ'ב'ה'	1910. May her soul be bound up in the bonds of eternal life.

63 – Chaim Baruch, son of Efraim Meir, 1 September 1908

חיים לן שבק והלך למעונתו
ברוך בצאתו ובבואו למנוחתו
במעשיו הטובים וישרתו
רק בתורה ועבודה כל מגמתו
עסק באמונה במלאכת שמים
השם ישלם שכרו כפלים
מוה" **חיים ברוך** בן מוה"
אפרים מאיר ז"ל נפטר
ה' אלול שנת תר"סח לפק
ת'נ'צ'ב'ה'

Chaim (Lan) died and went to his dwelling,
his departure is blessed and so is his arrival at his place of rest.
In his good deeds and his honesty,
studying the Torah and doing his work were his only goals.
He was faithfully occupied in godly work,
The Lord will reward him double.
Our teacher rav **Chaim Baruch**, son of our teacher rav
Efraim Meir, of blessed memory, passed away
on the 1st of September, of the year 1908.
May his soul be bound up in the bonds of eternal life.

השם היא תתהלל מ'
הינדה רבקה
בת מוה" **שמעי'** הכהן
ז"ל. נפטרה ז' ניסן
שנת תר"ע לפ'ק תנצב"ה

God. she will be praised, Mrs.
Hinda Ryvka,
daughter of our teacher the Rabbi **Shmay** HaKohen,
of blessed memory, passed away on the 16th of April
on the year 1910. May sher soul be bound up in the bonds of
eternal life.

65 – Yehoshua Ze'ev LIDAUER, son of Israel, 27 March 1909

פ"נ   Here is buried

איש הישר בדרכיו   A forthright man,

תמים במעשיו נהנה   fair in all his deeds. He enjoyed

מיגיע כפו ירא השם   the fruits of his labor. God-fearing,

מוה" **יהושע זאב** בן   our teacher the Rabbi **Yehoshua Ze'ev**, son of

מוה" **ישראל** ז"ל   our teacher the Rabbi **Israel**, of blessed memory,

לידאער נפטר יום ה   **Lidauer**, passed away on the 27th

ח' ניסן שנת תר'סט   of the month of March, on the year 1909.

66 – Golda Lea BRZEZINSKI, daughter of Yosef Shlomo, 15 June 1915

פ נ. מ' גאלדא לאה ברזעזינסקא
נפ בת ל'ג שנים ג' תמוז תר"עה
לפ'ק
אל מלא רחמים שוכן במרומים
המצא מנוחה נכונה על כנפי
השכינה במעלות קדושים וטהורים
בזוהר הרקיע מזהירים את נשמת
האישה **גולדה לאה** ב'ר **יוסף
שלמה**
שהלכה לעולמה בעבור שנדבו
צדקה בעד הזכרת נשמתה בגן עדן
תהא מנוחתה לכן בעל הרחמים
יסתירה בסתר כנפיו לעולמים ויצרור
בצרור החיים את נשמתה ד' היא
נחלתה
ותנוח בשלום על משכבה ונאמר
אמן

Here is buried Mrs. **Golda Leah Brzezinska**, passed away at 33 years old, on the 15th of June 1915

Merciful God, who dwells in the heavens,
provide a true rest on the wings of
the divine presence, aloft with the souls of the pure and holy
in the radiance of the heaven, brighten the soul of
the woman **Golda Leah**, daughter of reb **Yosef Shlomo**,

that passed away. Because of donating
to charity for memorial to her soul, in paradise
her rest should be, and for that the all-merciful
will shelter her in concealment of his wings forever, and will
bind up her soul in the bonds of eternal life, God, it is her
legacy.
May she rest in peace in her grave. And we'll say Amen.

67 – Yitzhak Yehuda, son of Abraham, 15 January 1912

תחת האבן הדומם ינוח
איש זקן נכבד ויקר רוח
ירא אלוקים והלך בתמים
נהנה מיגיע כפו כל הימים
מ' **יצחק יהודה** ב"ר
אברהם ז"ל נפטר כ'ה טבת
שנת תר"עב לפ'ק תנצ"ב
החיים

Under the inanimate stone rests
an old man, honorable and noble,
God-fearing and just.
He always enjoyed the fruits of his labor.
The late **Yitzhak Yehuda**, son of reb
Abraham, of blessed memory, passed away 15th of January
on the year 1912. May his soul be bound up in the bonds of
eternal life.

68 – (no name, woman)

פ נ	Here is buried
האישה היקרה	The dear woman,
צנועה וכשרה	modest and proper.
אתנו נעדרה __	She is missing from us
ובניה עזבה במרה	and her sons were left in bitterness.
אב שנת __ ____	Passed away on the __ of Av of the year ____
ת נ צ ב"ה	May her soul be bound up in the bonds of eternal life.

69 – Eliakum Getzel HOROWICZ, son of Moshe HaLevi, spouse of Chana HERSZKOWICZ, 26 November 1913

פ"נ איש צעיר לימים	Here is buried a young man
בכל שנותיו הלך תמים	His life was unblemished throughout,
ירא ד' מוה' **אליקום געצל**	God-fearing. Our teacher the rabbi **Elyakum Getzel**
בן מוה' **משה** הלוי	son of our teacher the rav **Moshe** HaLevi
הורוויץ	**Horowicz**,
נפטר כ'ו מרחשון שנ'	passed away on the 26th of November, of the year
תר'עד לפק תנצב"ה	1913. May his soul be bound up in the bonds of eternal life.

פה תנוח אישה יקרה
אשת חיל צנועה וכשרה
י"א נפש טהורה מרת
דבורה בת מוה' צבי ז"ל

Here rests a dear woman,
a modest and proper woman,
God-fearing pure soul. Mrs.
Dvora, daughter of our teacher the rav **Zvi**, of blessed
memory,

71 – Yehuda, son of Ozer HaKohen, 2 September 1914

פה	Here
ינוח איש ישר ותמים	rests an honest and unblemished man,
ירא השם כל הימים	God-fearing all his life
במבחר שנותיו עלה שמים	At the best years of his life, he went to heaven,
לאור שם לאור החיים	to God's light, to the light of life.
מוה" ר' **יהודה** ב"ר	Our teacher the rabbi reb **Yehuda**, son of
עוזר הכהן ז"ל נפט'	**Ozer** HaKohen, of blessed memory, passed away
י"א לחודש אלול	on the 2nd of the month of September
שנת תר'עד לפ'ק	of the year 1914.
ת נ צ ב ה"	May his soul be bound up in the bonds of eternal life.

72 – Moshe David, son of Gabriel, 6 March 1894

פ'נ	Here is buried
איש נכבד ומאושר אוהב צדקה	An honored and happy man, loves righteousness
וחסד מו' **משה דוד** בן מו' **גבריאל** ז'ל	and charity. Our teacher **Moshe David**, son of our teacher **Gabriel**, of blessed memory,
נפטר יום ך'ח אדר שני ש'תר"נד לפ'ק	passed away on the 6th of March, of the year 1894.

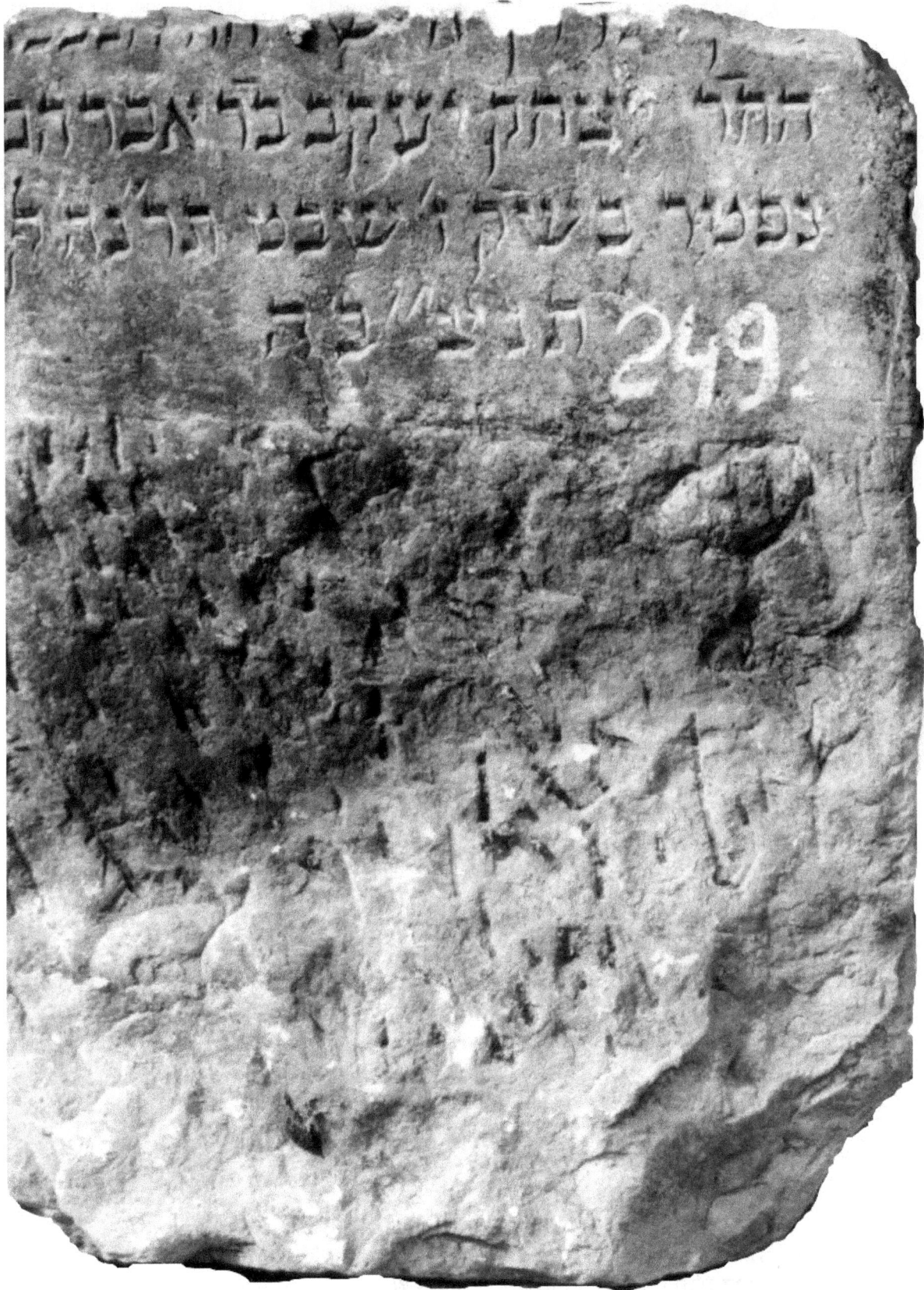

החו' יצחק יעקב בכר אברהם
נפטר בשק ושבת הרנה ל
תנצב 249

החֹ'ר **יצחק יעקב** ב'ר **אברהם**
נפטר בש'ק ז' שבט תר"נה לפ'ק
תנצ"בה

The sage reb **Yitzhak Yaakov**, son of reb **Abraham**,
passed away on Holy Shabbat, the 1st of February 1895.
May his soul be bound up in the bonds of eternal life.

פ' נ'	Here is buried
אשה נכבדה ויקרה	A dear and honorable woman,
אוהבת דרך ישרה	loving the righteous ways,
מהוללה במעשיה מ'	praised for her deeds. Mrs.
שרה יוטא בת מו'ר **אלי'**	**Sara Yuta** daughter of our teacher reb **Eliahu**,
נפ' ה' כסליו ש' תר"סו לפ'ק	passed away on the 3rd of December, of the year 1905.
ת נ צ " ב ה	May her soul be bound up in the bonds of eternal life.

75 – Ayzik CWANG, son of Chaim, spouse of Rachel ZYMER, 29 August 1896

מצבת ר' **איציק** ב'ר **חיים צוואנג** נפ' ר' אלול תר"נו לפ'ק

Gravestone of reb **Ayzik**, son of reb **Chaim Cwang**, passed away on 29th of August 1896.

פ'נ

Here is buried

איש נכבד תם וישר
כל מעשיו היו בכושר
מוה" **ישעיהו זאב** ב"ר
יוסף יעקב ז"ל נפטר
ג' אדר ב' תר'סח תנצבה

An honorable, unblemished and honest man,
was capable in all he did.
Our teacher the rav **Yeshayahu Ze'ev**, son of reb
Yosef Yaakov, of blessed memory, passed away on the
5th of February 1908. May his soul be bound up in the bonds
of eternal life.

77 – Chaya Malka, daughter of Efraim Fishel Kohen Tzedek, 8 November 1848

הוי' על אשר נחשך
בקרוב השמש בצהרים
כי נלקח מאיתנו ה"ה האישה
הצנועה המהוללה מרת
חי' מלכה בת המנוח
מהו' **אפרים פישל** כ"ץ
ז"ל נפטרת י"ב מרחשון
תר"ט לפ'ק תנצב"ה

Oy! for it darkened
when the sun approached noontime,
because taken from us was the very woman
that was modest and praised. Mrs.
Chaya Malka, daughter of the departed
our teacher **Efraim Fishel**, Kohen Tzedek
of blessed memory, passed away the 8th of November
1848. May her soul be bound up in the bonds of eternal life.

78 – Natan, son of Yeshayahu, 30 August 1873

איש תם וישר	An honest and upright man,
החבר ר' **נתן** בן	comrade reb **Natan**, son of
החבר ר' **ישעי'**	comrade reb **Yeshayahu**,
נפטר בשק' ז' אלול	passed away on Holy Shabbat, 30th of August
תר"לג תנצ"בה	1873. May his soul be bound up in the bonds of eternal life.

79 – Aharon Yaakov, son of Benyamin, 29 April 1895

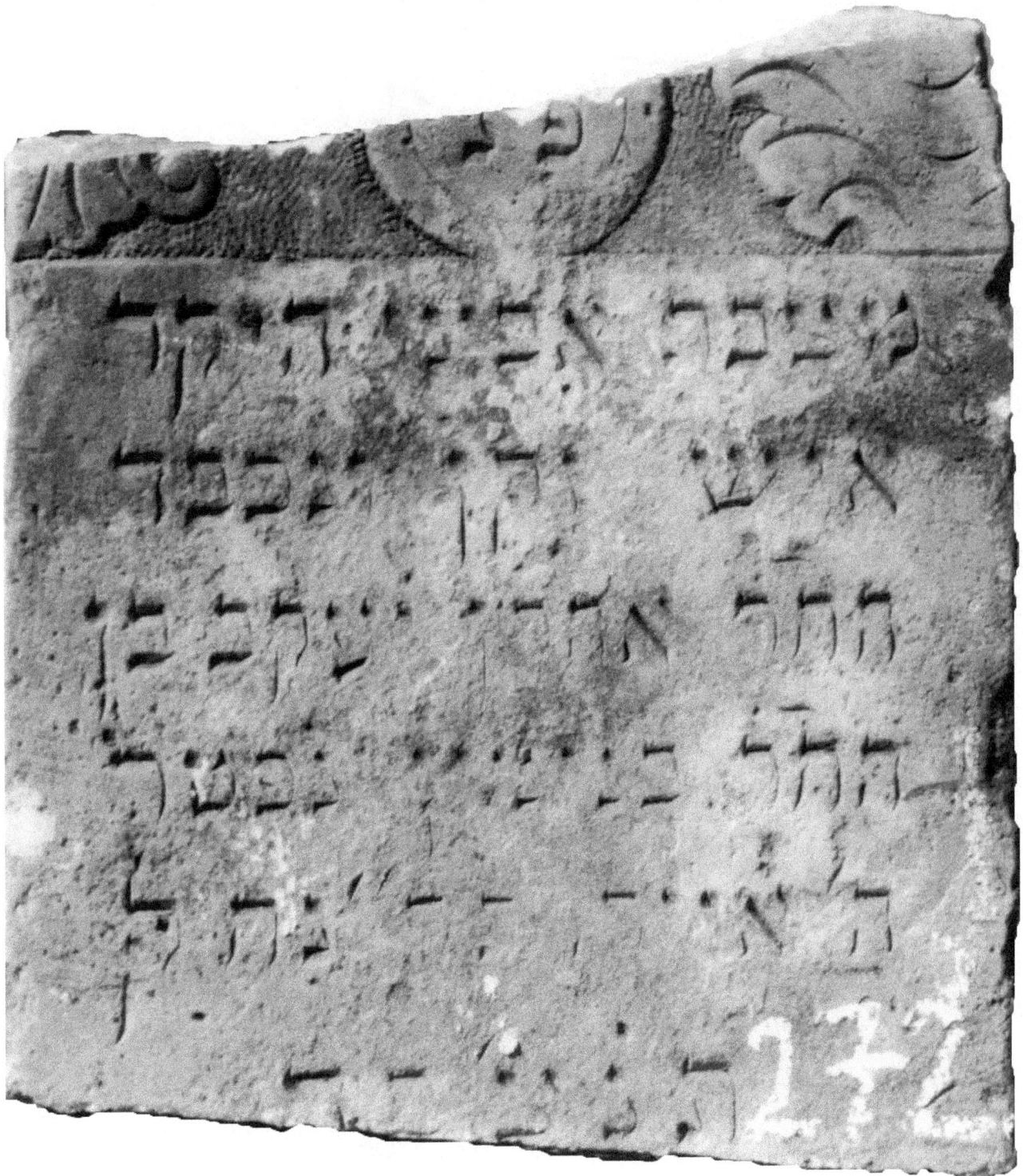

Gravestone of our dear father,	מצבת אבינו היקר
an old and honorable man.	איש זקן ונכבד
The sage reb **Aharon Yaakov**, son of	**הח'ר אהרון יעקב** בן
the sage reb **Benyamin**, passed away	הח'ר **בנימין** נפטר
on the 29th of April 1895.	ה' אייר תר"נה לפ'ק
May his soul be bound up in the bonds of eternal life.	תנצ"בה

80 – Avigdor WIGDOROWICZ, son of Moshe HaKohen, spouse of Gitel Leah ZAURBACH, 17 November 1912

פ'נ	Here is buried

איש הישר בדרכיו	An upright man,
תמים ـــــــ	honest ـــــــ
אלקים. נהנה מעמל	God, enjoyed the fruit of his
כפו מוה" **אביגדור** בן	labor. Our teacher the rabbi **Avigdor**, son of
מוה" **משה** הכהן ז"ל	our teacher the rabbi **Moshe** HaKohen, of blessed memory,
נפ' ז' כסליו תר'עג תנצ"בה	passed away on the 17th of November 1912. May his soul be bound up in the bonds of eternal life.

פ"נ האישה החשובה
אשת חיל יראת ה' מ'
גיטל לאה נאסעל
בת מוה" **משה אהרון**
נפטרה ה' כסליו שנ'
תר"עו לפ'ק תנצב"ה

Here is buried the important woman,
a woman of valor, God-fearing. Mrs.
Gitel Leah Nosal,
daughter of our teacher the rav **Moshe Aharon**,
passed away on the 12th of November of the year
1915. May her soul be bound up in the bonds of eternal life.

82 – Eliezer KOLSKI, son of Dov Ber, spouse of Tana LAJZEROWICZ, 22 February 1913

ירא _____	_____ fearing
ד' נהנה מיגיע כפיו	God, enjoyed the fruits of his labor.
מוה" **אליעזר** ב"ר	Our teacher the rabbi **Eliezer**, son of
דובער ז"ל נפט' ט"ו	**Dov Ber**, of blessed memory, passed away on the 22nd of
אדר ראשון שנת	February of the year
תר"עג לפ'ק תנצב"ה	1913. May his soul be bound up in the bonds of eternal life.

83 – Freida, daughter of Abraham, 28 June 1865

אישה זקנה וישרה	An old and honest woman.
מר' **פריידא** ב'ר	Mrs. **Freida**, daughter of
אברהם ז'ל	**Abraham**, of blessed memory,
נפטרה ד' תמוז תר"כה	passed away on the 28th of June 1865.
לפ'ק תנצ"בה	May her soul be bound up in the bonds of eternal life.

תם וישר ירא ד' — blameless and upright, God-fearing.
בתורה היה חפצתו — His pleasure was in the Torah.
ה'ה מוה' **חנינא זעליג** — This was the very one, our teacher the rabbi **Chanyna Zelig**,
בן מוה' **הילל** ז'ל — son of our teacher the rav **Hillel**, of blessed memory,
גוע בש'ט יום ה' י' — died in a good name on Thursday 24th of
טבת תר'כט לפ'ק — December 1868.
ת'נ'צ'ב'ה' — May his soul be bound up in the bonds of eternal life.

85 – Chaya Roza, daughter of Yitzhak Ayzik, 8 June 1892

הי‎ _‏ _‏ונא‎ _____	_____
כחצי‎ _‏ י'‎ הה‎ נעדרה	_____ was missing
וי‎ ונהי‎ עלנו‎ נפלה‎ הצרה	Woe and wail, calamity befell us.
נכבדה‎ וישרה‎ אומללה	Honorable and upright, wretched
אשה‎ צנועה‎ ומהוללה	modest and praised woman.
מרת‎ **חי'‎ רוזא‎** בת‎ הר'ר	Mrs. **Chaya Roza**, daughter of the Rabbi
יצחק‎ אייזיק‎ נ'י‎ נ'‎ ביום‎ ה'	**Yitzhak Ayzik**, may his light shine, passed away on Thursday
כ'א‎ סיון‎ תר'מב‎ תנצ'בה	8th of June 1882. May her soul be bound up in the bonds of eternal life.

86 – ?, spouse of Abraham KOLSKI, 19 July 1894

פ"נ האשה הכשרה	Here is buried the proper woman,
חשובה וצנועה	important and modest,
יראת ד' ___	God-fearing ____.
מ' ___ א'ר **אברהם**	Mrs. _____, wife of reb **Abraham**
קאלסקי נפ ט'ו אלול	**Kolski**, passed away on the 19th of July, on the
שנ' תר'נד לפ'ק תנצב"ה	year 1894. May her soul be bound up in the bonds of eternal life.

87 – Shlomo, son of Yitzhak Ayzik, 26 July 1921

פ נ   Here is buried

אבינו היקר איש נכבד   our dear father, an honorable man.
שלמה ב'ר יצחק אייזיק   **Shlomo**, son of reb **Yitzhak Ayzik**,
נפטר כ' תמוז ש' תר'פא   passed away on the 26th of July, on the year 1921.
לפ'ק
תנצ"בה   May his soul be bound up in the bonds of eternal life.

88 – Tova Sara SOSNOWSKI, daughter of Abraham HaKohen, 10 May 1915

פ"נ האשה החשובה
כשרה וצנועה יראת ה'
היא תתהלל מרת
טאבא שרה
סאסנאווסקי
בת ר' **אברהם** הכהן
נפ' כ"ו אייר ש' תר"עה
לפ'ק ת נ צ ב " ה

Here is buried the important woman,
proper and modest, God-fearing.
She is praised. Mrs.
Tova Sara
Sosnowski,
daughter of reb **Avraham** HaKohen,
passed away on the 10th of May, of the year 1915.
May her soul be bound up in the bonds of eternal life.

89 – Shlomo, son of Eliakum Eliezer

Here is buried a faithful man, reb **Shlomo**, son of reb **Eliakum Eliezer** __

פ' נ' איש אמונים ר' **שלמה** ב'ר
אליקום אליעזר __

90 – Asher Eli__, son of Mordechai HaLevi, 10 November 1902

פ"נ	Here is buried
איש נכבד ויקר רוח	A man, honorable and dear soul,
נדיב לב ומרבה צדקה	generous of heart and in charity
וחסד לרש	and kindness to the poor.
הה הרבני _____	_____
מו'ה **אשר אלי__** בן	our teacher the rav **Asher Eli__**, of blessed memory, son of
מו'ה **מרדכי** הלוי ז"ל	our teacher the rav **Mordechai** HaLevi, of blessed memory,
נפטר י' חשון ש' תר"סג לפ'ק	passed away on the 10th of November, on the year 1902.
ת נ צ"ב ה	May his soul be bound up in the bonds of eternal life.

איש ישר ותמים	An honest and unblemished man,
ירא השם כל הימים	God-fearing all his days,
מ' **משה חיים** ב'ר דוד	The late **Moshe Chaim**, son of reb **David**
ליכטענשטיין	**Lichtensztajn**,
נפ' כ"ז אייר תר'עה	passed away on the 11th of May 1915.
תנצבה	May his soul be bound up in the bonds of eternal life.

92 – (no name, woman)

נ" האשה החשובה

כשרה וצנועה

יראת ה' היא תתהלל

Here is buried the important woman,

modest and proper,

God-fearing, she will be praised.

93 – Zvi Hirsh KOZAK, son of Michael, spouse of Mindel KINCLER
19 December 1900

קוננים	Mourning
_____	_____
צבי הירש __א אבינו	**Zvi Hirsh** _____ our father
מי_____	_____
כי נפלה על ראשינו	for befell on our heads.
אהה פתאם עלה שמים	Ah! Suddenly he went to the sky,
לרעות בגנה בארץ החיים	to stroll in the garden of the eternal life,
איש נכבד אהב עשות	an honorable man who loved doing
חסד מוה' **צבי הירש** ב' מו'	good. Our teacher the rav **Zvi Hirsh**, son of our teacher
מיכאל נפט' יום ך'ז כסליו	**Michael**, passed away on the 19th of December of the
ש' תר"סא תנצ"בה	year 1900. May his soul be bound up in the bonds of eternal life.

94 – Moshe, son of Yechezkel HaLevi, 17 August 1879

מ' **משה** ב"ר **יחזקאל** הלוי ז'ל
נ' ונ' ביום א' רח' מנחם אב
שנת תר"לט לפ'ק
תנצ"בה

Our teacher **Moshe** son of reb **Yechezkel** HaLevi,
passed away and was buried on Sunday, the 17th of August
of the year 1879.
May his soul be bound up in the bonds of eternal life.

האשה **רחל לאה**	The woman **Rachel Leah**,
בת ר' **יצחק קראוער**	daughter of reb **Yitzhak Krauer**,
נפ' ז' אב תר"לג לפ'ק	passed away on the 31st of July 1873.

97 – Yosef

פה נטמן אדם _____	Here is interred an honest man,
יגע ועמל כל ימיו _____	toiled and labored all his days ___
ודובר אמת ואין _____	and spoke truthfully.
ספדו דלים כי	Mourn, you poor, because he
פזר נדבות לכל _____	dispersed alms to all the needy.
ערע_____	_____

98 – Henich, son of Shmuel Ze'ev, 20 September 1901

ומאושר ה'ה	And happy, the very one
העניך בן ה'ה	**Henich**, son of the very one
שמואל זאב נ'י	**Shmuel Ze'ev**, may his light shine,
נפטר עש'ק ז' תשרי	passed away on the eve of holy Shabbat, 20th of September
תר"סב	1901.

99 – Eliezer TORONCZYK

פ'נ	Here is buried
אליעזר טאראנטשיק	**Eliezer Toronczyk**
פ"נ	Here is buried
הבחור הנכבד	the honorable young man,
בעל ____ע טוב	husband _____ good

100 – Feiga SZWARC, wife of Aharon David, 20 May 1936

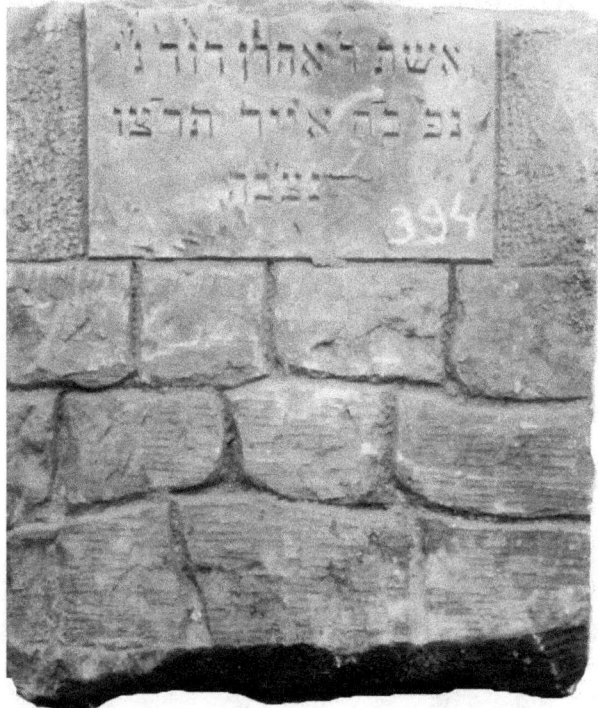

מ' פייגא שווארץ	Mrs. **Feiga Szwarc**
פ'נ	Here is buried
אמנו היקרה ונכבדה	Our dear and honored mother
פייגא	**Feiga**
שווארץ	**Szwarc,**
אשת **אהרן דוד** נ'י	wife of **Aharon David**, may his light shine,
נפ' כ'ח אייר תר"צו	passed away on the 20th of May 1936.
תנצ"בה	May her soul be bound up in the bonds of eternal life.

דינה אש	**Dina Asz**
דא לב _____	This heart _____
יבכו פני על ___ השבר	My face will cry for the bitter heartbreak
נפלה עטרת ראשנו, כי	the crown of our head has fallen, as
הכשרה בנשים אפ _ כנפי	the most proper of women _____
בת _____ השנים	_____
רב צדקה וחסד דרכה	Much charity and kindness _____
אפרים סאכאטשאוער ז"ל	**Efraim Sochaczower**, of blessed memory,
נפטרה י'א חשון תר'צא	passed away on 2nd of November 1930
תנצ'בה	May her soul be bound up in the bonds of eternal life.

102 – Zvi, son of Moshe, 13 December 1877

עטרת **צבי**   **Zvi**'s Crown

ציון קבר איש תמים   Marking of an unblemished man,
וישר הלך כל (ה)ימים   upright throughout his life.
(דאג?) לפרנס ב'ב באמונה   Took care to provide his family faithfully
(וב)כבד ירא ד' אהב תבונה   and honestly. God-fearing; loved knowledge.
כר' **צבי** בר' **משה** ז"ל   The honorable reb **Zvi**, son of reb **Moshe**, of blessed
נפטר ביום ד' ו' טבת   memory,
שנת תר"לח לפ'ק   passed away on Wednesday, 12th of December on the year
1877.
תנצ"בה   May his soul be bound up in the bonds of eternal life.

103 – Abraham, son of Yitzhak, 17 July 1910

פ"נ איש הישר בדרכיו
תמים במעשיו ירא אלקים
נהנה מיגיע כפו מוה"ר
אברהם בן מוה"ר **יצחק**
ז"ל נפטר י' תמוז שנ'
תר"ע לפ'ק תנצב"ה

Here is buried an upright man,
unblemished in his deeds and God-fearing,
who enjoyed the fruits of his labor. Our teacher the rabbi
Abraham son of our teacher the rabbi **Yitzhak**,
of blessed memory, passed away on the 17th of July, on the year
1910. May his soul be bound up in the bonds of eternal life.

104 – Mirel, daughter of Yaakov, 19 April 1869

מהוללת אשה בשנים רכה	Praised us a young woman,
יראת ה טהורה כלבונה זכה	God-fearing, immaculate and pure like frankincense.
כל יודעיה צדקת וישרה	All knew her to be saintly and honest,
ב'מותה יבכו ולה _____	will cry at her death _____
(ד'? ה'?) יועלו על _ מר_	_____
בת **יעקב** _____	daughter of Yaakov _____
את הצנועה מר' **מירלה**	The modest Miss **Mira'le**,
בת הרבני מו'ר **יעקב** נ'י	daughter of the Rabbi, our teacher the rav **Yaakov**, may his light shine,
נפטרה יום ב' ח' אייר תר"כט לפ'ק	passed away on Monday 19th of April 1869.
תנצב"ה	May her soul be bound up in the bonds of eternal life.

105 – Moshe, son of Shlomo, 24 April 1886

פ' נ'	Here is buried
אדם נכבד חמדת הוריו	an honored man, the joy of his parents.
הלך בדרך הישר	He followed the righteous ways.
ר' **משה** בן החבר _____	_____ reb **Moshe**, son of comrade
ר' **שלמה** ז"ל	reb **Shlomo**, of blessed memory;
נפטר ביום ד' דחו'המ' פסח	passed away on the 24th of April
תר"מו לפ'ק	of the year 1886.
תנצ"בה	May his soul be bound up in the bonds of eternal life.

106 – Gela, daughter of David, 20 August 1852

ג//עי במ(ותה), ובכי על אב(דן)

Wail at her death and cry for the loss

ע__ וקוננו על קיצה המר

____ and mourn her bitter end.

לוא היתר לבי על נס צלליך

My heart did not permit your shadows to flee

איך אנחם וכל ילדיך

How will I console all your children

על פטירת אשת חיל

on the passing away woman of valor,

ה/ה' האישה הצנו"(עה) במעש"(ה)

the very woman who was modest in her deeds?

תם דרכי'(ה) כ"פלעני מרת

Her roads are no more. _____ Mrs.

געלא בת המנ"(וח) מה"ו **דוד**

Gela, daughter of our teacher the reb **David**,

ז"ל. נו"נ יום ח' לחודש אלול

of blessed memory, died and buried on the 20th of August, of

ש'(נת) תר"יב ת נ צ ב ה

the year 1852. May her soul be bound up in the bonds of eternal life.

107 – Ite Bracha FRENKEL, 1892-1937

Here is buried	פ"נ
Ite Bracha Frenkel	**יטע ברכה פרענקעל**
Here rests	דא רוען
our unforgettable	אונזער נישטפארגעסעלכע
and beloved dear	און טייער געשעצטע
mother and wife	מוטער און פרוי
Ite Bracha	**יטע ברכה**
____ ___baum	**בוים___ ___ ____**
born on _____ 1892	תר'נב _____
passed away on _____ 1937	תר'צז _____

פ"נ   Here is buried

אסתר שיינא ווינער   **Ester Sheina Winer**

109 – Ester, daughter of Yehuda Leib, 3 July 1873

אישה יראת ד' היא תתהלל	A God-fearing woman, she will be praised.
סחרה טוב מסחר כסף.הלכ(ה)	Her knowledge in business is more valuable than just for the money. Her ways
תמה עם א'קי' (אלקים) ואנשים	unblemished with God and people.
רכה בשנים חלקה בשמים	Young in years, [she is in] her portion in heaven,
הה הצנועה היקרה	Alas. The dear, modest
והישרה מר' **אסתר** בת	and honest Mrs. **Ester**, daughter of
מו'ה **יהודא ליב** ז"ל	our teacher the rav **Yehuda Leib**, of blessed memory,
נפטרה ח' תמוז תר"לג	passed away on the 3rd of July 1873.
לפק תנצבה	May her soul be bound up in the bonds of eternal life.

פ"נ הבתולה מ' **רעכל**
ראצא בת ר' **חיים** נ"י
נפט' ט'ז טבת שנת
תר"עב לפ'ק תנצבה

Here is buried the maiden, Ms **Rechel Ratza**, daughter of reb **Chaim**, may his light shine, passed away on the 5th of January, on the year 1912. May her soul be bound up in the bonds of eternal life.

111 – Chana Liba ARBUS, daughter of Asher Anchel

פ"נ האישה החשובה
כשרה וצנועה יראת ה'
מ' **חנה ליבא ארבוס**
בת מוה' **אשר אנטשל**

Here is buried the important woman,
proper and modest. God-fearing
Mrs. **Chana Liba Arbus**,
daughter of our teacher the rav **Asher Anchel**,

פ'נ'	Here is buried
איש ככלח לקבר בא	A man, brought to the grave like an obsolete husk,
לבתי חומר נפש דאה	To clay houses, a soul is gliding.
יעיד דרכו נאמנה	Direct his way faithfully.
עלע לרגבי אדמה	As a rock to clods of earth,
ז____שבע ימים	_____ of days
ר____	_____

113 – Roza, daughter of Shimon, 29 June 1841

ה"ה מ' **רוזה** בת המנו(ח)	Woe! **Roza**, daughter of the deceased
מ' **שמעון** ז"ל נפט'ון	The late **Shimon**, of blessed memory, died and was buried
ביום י' תמוז תר"א לפ'ק	on the day 29th of June 1841.
ת' נ' צ' ב' ה'	May her soul be bound up in the bonds of eternal life.

114 – Aharon, son of Michael, 30 November 1870

פ נ	Here is buried
איש אמונים הולך תום	A faithful, upright man,
הה' **אהרון** נאסף פתאום	the learned rabbi **Aharon**, was gathered suddenly.
רב בשנים נחשך אורנו	He was old. Our light has been darkened,
____ בחוצות זעקת שברו	_____ heartbreaking cry in the streets.
ה"ה ד'הר' **אהרון** ב___	__ of the rabbi **Aharon B__** son of
ר' **מיכאל** ז"ל נפטר	reb **Michael**, of blessed memory, passed away
ר'ו כסליו שנת	on the 30th of November, on the year
תר"לא לפ'ק תנ"צבה	1870. May his soul be bound up in the bonds of eternal life.

115 – Sara Rachel, daughter of Abraham Zvi HaLevi, 8 May 1876

פ נ האישה הצנועה
במעשי(ה) יראת ה'
אשת חיל מ' **שרה**
רחל בת **אברהם צבי**
הלוי. נפ' י'ד אייר
ש' תר"לו תנצבה"

Here is buried the woman modest in
her deeds and God-fearing,
a woman of valor. Mrs. **Sara
Rachel**, daughter of **Abraham Zvi**
HaLevi, passed away on the 8th of May of the
year 1876. May her soul be bound up in the bonds of eternal
life.

116 – Yosef Zvi, son of Abraham Yoel, 13 July 1924

אִיש ישר דרך וירא	A righteous, God-fearing man
לילות וימים ____	____ days and nights.
ר' **יוסף צבי**	Reb **Yosef Zvi**,
ב'ר **אברהם יואל**	son of reb **Abraham Yoel**,
נפטר ביום י"א תמוז	passed away on the 13th of July,
שנת תר"פד לפ'ק	on the year 1924.

117 – (no name), January or February 1916

שבט תר"עו תנצבה   (January/February) 1916

118 – Golda

ה'ה!	Woe!
מאוד זעקו עלי	Lots cried for me
____הֹתי ומכירי	_____ and my acquaintances
על האישה רכה בשנים	on the young woman
גאלדא	**Golda**

מ' שרה יאקובאוויטש   Mrs. **Sara Jakubowicz**

פ'נ   Here is buried
אישה רכה בשנים   a young woman
הלכה מאיתנו   who left us_____

120 – (no name)

ציון לנפש חיה	A monument to a living soul
חשכת קודר ____	_____ somber darkness
ים ונודר_____	_____ and vow
ך_____	_____

121 – Gitel Rajzel FUKS

גיטל רייזל פוקס   **Gitel Rayzel Fuks**

פ'נ   Here is buried

122 – (no name, woman)

123 – Ester, daughter of Yaakov, 2 June 1902

A _____ and important woman   אישה ___ וחשובה
_____   _____ כל _____

_____   _____

_____   _____

Ester, daughter of reb **Yaakov**,   אסתר ב'ר יעקב
passed away on the 2nd of June 1902.   נפ כ'ו אייר תר"סב
May her soul be bundled in the bundle of life.   ת נ צ ב ה

חוה רויזא ראזענבערג	**Chava Royza Rozenberg**
~~	~~~~~~~~~~~~~~~~
פ'נ	Here is buried
אישה צעירה ורכה בשנים	a young and tender woman
עולליה ____ מר יזעקון	her children crying bitterly
אימנו הלכה ואתנו עזבה	our mother went and left us.
חוה רויזא	**Chava Royza**
ב'ר **יעקב**	daughter of reb **Yaakov**
נפ' י'ז שבט תר"פג	passed away on the 3rd of January 1923.
ת' נ' צ' ב' ה'	May her soul be bound up in the bonds of eternal life.

פ'נ	Here is buried
נאשא פאסטערנאק	**Nasha Pasternak**,
ב'ר בער ליב	daughter of **Ber Leib**,
נפ' ז' אלול תר'פח	passed away on the 23rd of August 1928.

126 – Adel WITKOWSKI, daughter of Mendel, 27 August 1923

אדעל וויטקאווסקי   **Adel Witkowski**

פ'נ   Here lies

בחללה מאיתנו אמנו   _____ from us
היקרה והישרה   our dear and fair mother,
נזר ראשנו ומחמדנו   the beloved crown of our head.
אדעל   **Adel**,
ב'ר מענדעל   daughter of reb **Mendel**,
נפ' ט'ו אלול תר"פג   passed away on the 27ᵗʰ of August 1923.
ת נ צ ב ה   May her soul be bound up in the bonds of eternal life

127 – Beila BLAWAT, daughter of Reuven, 18 May 1911

ביילה בלאוואט	**Beila Blawat**
פ'נ	Here is buried
ציון לנפש אשה תמימה	A monument to an innocent woman
_____ ורוח נדיבה	_____ and a generous spirit.
פרשה לעניים כפיה	She stretched her hands to the needy.
ביילה ב'ר **ראובן** ז"ל	**Beila**, daughter of reb **Reuven**, of blessed memory,
נפ' כ' אייר תר'עא	passed away on the 18th of May 1911.
ת נ צ ב ה	May her soul be bound up in the bonds of eternal life.

בינה יאקאבאויטש	**Bina Jakobowicz**
במות אמנו היקרה	The day our dear mother died
יום צרה עלינו היה	was a day of woe for us.
נשמתה בצדה תהי צרורה	Her soul at her side will be bundled.
בינה	**Bina**,
ב'ר _____	daughter of _____,
נפ' כ'ה ____	passed away on the 25th of _____
ת נ צ ב ה	May her soul be bound up in the bonds of eternal life.

**129 – Zvi Matityahu FRENKIEL, son of Shlomo,
spouse of Liba GOLDMAN, 24 December 1926**

‏רנו על בשרנו___‏	We felt it on our bodies
‏נילקח מאתנו מורנו‏	Taken from us was our teacher.
‏היקר והנכבד‏	The dear and honorable
‏צבי מתיהו‏	**Zvi Matityahu**,
‏ב'ר **שלמה**‏	son of **Shlomo**

ר' יחיאל מאבל גאנשער	Reb **Yechiel Mabel Ganszer**
פ'נ	Here is buried
פלגי מים תרד עינינו	Our eyes will run streams of water
בזכרנו את שברנו	when remembering our heartbreak,
___ לה עטרת ראשנו	the crown of our heads has fallen.
המקום ינחם אותנו	God will console us.
יחיאל מאבל	**Yechiel Mabel**
ב'ר **יהודה ליב** ז"ל	son of **Yehuda Leib**, of blessed memory,
נפ' כ'ו אדר ב' תר'עט	passed away on the 28th of March 1919.
ת נ צ ב ה	May his soul be bound up in the bonds of eternal life.

131 – (no name)

תנצבה   May his/her soul be bound up in the bonds of eternal life.

132 – ?, 18 January 1893

נפ ר'ח שבט תר'נג   passed away on the 18th of January 1893.
ת'נ'צ'ב'ה'   May his/her soul be bound up in the bonds of eternal life.

133 – Abraham Yitzhak GRINBAUM, son of Yehuda Leibush and Gitel Leah

חבל על דאבדין	A pity for those lost
פ"נ	Here is buried
ולא משתכחין	but will not be forgotten.
אברהם יצחק	**Abraham Yitzhak**
ב"ר **יהודה ליבוש ופריל לאה**	son of **Yehuda Leibush** and **Perel Leah**
גרינבוים	**Grinbaum**.
נ"ע	May his soul dwell in paradise.
_____ צר ל _____	_____

מ' **צפורה סימע קארן**	Mrs. **Tzipora Sima Korn**
פ"נ	Here is buried
אשה רכה בשנים	a young woman.
יילילו עמנו כל אנשים	Howl with us, all people,
על השבר אשר קרנו	for the heartbreak that befell us
מ' **צפורה סימע**	Mrs. **Tzipora Sima**
ב'ר **יצחק מאיר פערעץ**	daughter of reb **Yitzhak Meir Perec**,
נ"פ כ"ז אייר תר"צב	passed away on the 5th of March 1932.
ת נ צ ב ה	May her soul be bound up in the bonds of eternal life.

135 – Tane KOLSKI, daughter of Asher LAJZEROWICZ, wife of Leizer KOLSKI, 13 June 1918

טאנע

ב'ר אשר ז'ל

נפ' ג' תמוז תר"עח ת'נ'צ'ב'ה'

Tane

daughter of reb **Asher**, of blessed memory,
passed away on the 13th of June 1918. May her soul be
bound up in the bonds of eternal life.

Tauba Sara Bugalski　　טויבה שרה בוגאלסקי

Here is buried　　פ'נ

For the heartbreak that befell us,　　לשבר אשר קראנו
cry with us and with our family,　　יזעקו עמנו ומשפחתנו
____ was taken from us.　　נילקחה מאיתנו __

137 – Chaya Leah RAK

Chaya Leah Rak   חיה לאה ראק

Here is buried.   פ"נ
A monument to the soul of a righteous woman   ציון לנפש אישה תמימה

138 – Leah, daughter of Shimon

ספונה פה לעיניך ___	____ concealed here from your eyes.
היא בנעורי בית אבי שבה	She, in my youth, to my father's home, returned.
לשמע תצלינה אזניך	Hearing the news, your ears will ring.
ה'ה האשה הצנועה ויקרה	Alas! The dear and humble woman
ממשפחה נכבדה ומפוארה	from an honorable and glorious family,
בגזע קדושים מהודרת	of a blessed descent
מ' **לאה** ז'ל בת הרב המא'הג'	Mrs. **Leah**, of blessed memory, daughter of the Rabbi "the great light"
מו'ה **שמעון** נ'י א'ב'ד'ק' **אברזיצק**	our teacher the rav **Shimon**, may his light shine, president of the Holy Court of the community of Obrzycko.
ת נ צ ב ה	May her soul be bound up in the bonds of eternal life.

139 – Yehoshua KRENIK, son of Yitzhak Yaakov, spouse of Perla WARSZAWSKI

_____ תם וישר	_____ unblemished and upright,
יהושע בן	**Yehoshua**, son of
יצחק יעקב ז"ל	**Yitzhak Yaakov**, of blessed memory,
קרעניק	**Krenik**.
ת נ צ ב ה	May his soul be bound up in the bonds of eternal life.

140 – Ryvka, daughter of Shmuel, June or July 1928

האישה החשובה __	____ the important woman,
____ולה ויקרה	_____ and dear,
פתירה ____ _	_ ___ _____
מ' **רבקה**	Mrs **Ryvka**,
בת **שמואל**	daughter of **Shmuel**,
תמוז תר'פח ____	passed away in (June or July) 1928.

141 – Pesa SZTARK

מ' פעסא שטארק   Mrs. **Pesa Sztark**

142 – (no name)

```
____ית צ____
____ה קרא
תנצבה
```

פה תנוח האשה רכה

בשנים חשובה וצנוע(ה)

יראת ה' אשת חיל מ'

צפורה פעריל ב"ר

אברהם אבא הלוי נפ'

תר__ ___ __ ת'נ'צ'ב'ה'

Here rests a young woman
Important and modest,
God fearing, a woman of valor. Mrs.
Tzipora Perel, daughter of reb
Abraham Aba HaLevi, passed away on the
_____. May her soul be bound up in the bonds of eternal life.

144 – Liba FRENKIEL, daughter of Matitiahu GOLDMAN, wife of (Matys) Hirsh, 20 May 1901

רכה בשנים מ' **ליבא** בת
ר' **מתתיהו** נ'י **גאלדמאן** אשת
ר' **הירש פרענקעל** שלוח לעפרה
נפטרה יום ב' סיון ש' תר"סא לפ'ק
ת נ צ" ב ה

in tender age. Mrs. **Liba**, daughter of
reb **Matityahu Goldman**, may his light shine, wife of
reb **Hirsh Frenkel**, was sent to her grave,
passed away on 20th of May of the year 1901.
May her soul be bound up in the bonds of eternal life.

שאו קינה על השבר   Cry woe for the heartbreak!
על מות פתאום זה הגבר   for the sudden death of this man.
איש נכבד רך בשנים   An honorable young man,
יתומים השאיר עולי ימים   left behind orphans,
אהב עשות חסד הה מוה   loved doing charity. The very one, our teacher the rabbi
משה יעקב ב'ר דוד יהודא נ'י   **Moshe Yaakov** son of reb **David Yehuda**, may his light shine,

נפטר ביום ר'ח שבט תר"נו לפ'ק   passed away on the 16th of January 1896.
ת נ צ" ב ה   May his soul be bound up in the bonds of eternal life.

146 – Foygel LUKS, daughter of Hersh GRDUK, wife of David Shlomo, 25 December 1906

ה' פויגל אשת ר' **דוד שלמה לוקס**
נ'י

Mrs. **Foygel**, wife of reb **David Shlomo Luks**, may his light shine.

ספדו בקול מרה
הה! כי גועה ונעדרה
אשת נכבדה וישרה
לעני פרשה כפיה
אין אונים תמכה בידיה
ה' **פויגל** _____

Mourn in a bitter voice.
Woe! Because she died and is missed,
a righteous and honest woman,
who opened her hand to the needy
and to the helpless handed support.
Mrs. **Foygel**, _____

147 – (no name, woman)

שיינה עידעלמאן   **Sheina Eidelman**

פ'נ   Here is buried
אשה רכה בשנים   A woman young in years

Eismanowicz
Died on 18th of December
1928

150 – Dora Glika, daughter of Moshe Zvi

She guided her children in the ways of the Torah,
She was careful to follow God's commands.
A woman of valor, God-fearing.
The modest and honest Mrs.
Dora Glika,
daughter of reb **Moshe Zvi**, of blessed memory, _____
_____ passed away

הדריכה בני בדרכי התורה
במצות ד' היתה נזהרה
אשת חיל יראת ד'
הצנועה והכשרה מרת
דורא גליקא
ב'ר **משה צבי** ז'ל ____
נפטרה ____

151 – Sara Leah JACHIMOWICZ

פ'נ מ' **שרה לאה**
יאכימאוויטש

שומו שמים על שברנו
ראש היתה למשפחתנו
האשה הצנועה
לא נשכחת מלבנו

א_____
ה_____

Here is buried Mrs. **Sara Leah Jachimowicz**.

Heaven, woe for our calamity!
She was the head of our family.
The modest woman
is not forgotten from our heart.

Yitzhak Pinchas
Kaubec

יצחק פינחס
קאובעץ

_____   _____
                         __ לקברתה ולא נשאר

_____   _____
passed away on the 5th of Nisan ____. May her soul be   נפ' ה' ניסן תר"__ תנצבה
bound up in the bonds of eternal life.

ר' אלימלך הירשביין   Mr. **Elimelech Hirszbajn**

פ״נ   Here is buried
א׳ש תם ׳שר   An upright and honest man

655

אברהם יצחק זיסלינג   **Abraham Yitzhak Zysling**

פ״נ   Here is buried

660

ליבען טאר=אנטשיק

ליבע טאראנטשיק   Liba Toronczyk

156 – Rachel, daughter of Menachem

פ נ   Here is buried

רחל עמנו נלקחת מאתנו   Our mother Rachel was taken away from us.
חן מצאה לכל יודעיה   She was liked by all who knew her.
לצל צדקניות ד' יסתירה   God will hide her by the shade of the righteous women.
רחל   **Rachel**
בת ר' **מנחם** ז'ל   daughter of reb **Menachem**, of blessed memory,

157 – (no name, woman), 1921 or 1922

האשה _____ יקרת הרוח	The noble woman ____
פה אוצר נישמתנו תנוח	Here is where our soul's treasure rests.
כל יודעיה יבואו יתאבלו	All her acquaintances will come and mourn
על אירו____ל כבודנו כי ולו	for the _____
נפ' ____ תר"פב	passed away on ____ (1921 or 1922)
ת נ צ ב ה	May her soul be bundled in the bundle of life.

158 – (no name, woman)

פישער ____ מ'   Mrs. ____ **Fiszer**

חן מצאה לכל יודעיה   All her acquaintances found her pleasing